FEAR OF FLYING SOLO

FEAR OF FLYING SOLO

An Empowering Guide to Recovery from Divorce

Marsha Vaughn

NEW YORK

LONDON • NASHVILLE • MELBOURNE • VANCOUVER

FEAR OF FLYING SOLO
An Empowering Guide to Recovery from Divorce

Published in New York, New York, by Morgan James Publishing in partnership with Difference Press. Morgan James is a trademark of Morgan James, LLC. www.MorganJamesPublishing.com

The Morgan James Speakers Group can bring authors to your live event. For more information or to book an event visit The Morgan James Speakers Group at www.TheMorganJamesSpeakersGroup.com.

ISBN 9781642790115 paperback
ISBN 9781642790122 eBook
Library of Congress Control Number: 2018936335

Cover and Interior Design by:
Christopher Kirk
www.GFSstudio.com

In an effort to support local communities, raise awareness and funds, Morgan James Publishing donates a percentage of all book sales for the life of each book to Habitat for Humanity Peninsula and Greater Williamsburg.

Get involved today! Visit
www.MorganJamesBuilds.com

ADVANCE PRAISE

"*Fear of Flying Solo: An Empowering Guide to Recovery from Divorce,* by Marsha Vaughn, wastes no time offering a trauma-informed approach to healing on every page. Her direct experience, therapeutic skills, and lucid writing make this book useful to anyone recovering from divorce or trauma."

—Gerald Chambers, LMFT
Author of *The Pocket Anger Manager*

"A must-read for anyone, especially women, who are recently divorced. In *Fear of Flying Solo: An Empowering Guide to Recovery from Divorce,* Marsha provides deeply felt, authentic, and helpful guidance to get through this confusing and overwhelming time. Through the process of her own healing and transition from one identity (married) to another (divorced) and to another (single), Marsha lays out practical steps, exercises, tools, resources, and emotional support for a journey that no one signs up for, and so many must undertake, often unexpectedly! You won't have to fear flying solo anymore with Marsha's words and guidance by your side."

—Schelli Whitehouse
Equine Alchemy Certified Coach and Facilitator
Author of *The Business of Coaching with Horses*

"Going through a divorce – or even contemplating the idea – is extraordinarily difficult. In *Fear of Flying Solo*, Marsha Vaughn brings light to an often dark path with humor, compassion, and just the right amount of guidance. Using examples from her own life and those she has coached, Marsha has created a clear framework to navigate this life transition with grace. This book will top my recommended reading list for sure!"

—Kristina Hallett, PhD, ABPP
Board Certified Clinical Psychologist
Executive Coach
Author of *Own Best Friend: Eight Steps to a Life of Purpose, Passion, and Ease*

*This book is dedicated to my dad, Eldred Mowery, Jr.,
who wanted to be an author and believed in me—
no matter what.*

TABLE OF CONTENTS

Introduction
"HOUSTON, WE HAVE A PROBLEM"

The rose flower opens in the morning; by the evening the petals have dropped, withered away, gone back to rest in the earth. That does not mean that the rose flower was unreal.

– Osho

You can't believe you are divorced, can you? How did you get *here?* Some of the things you are thinking right now sound like this: "I thought I was married for life. I believed in that 'until death do us part' stuff and made a vow before God and all of my friends and family. I have so failed. I can't believe this. I was single for so long before I met him. I thought I was done with that!"

You did everything you could to make it work. Maybe you followed everyone else's suggestions, too – like: see a counselor, dress differently, have more fun time, have more "me" time. None of it worked. Now here you are. Wondering how this happened. Even though you may have partially wanted it. You knew somewhere deep inside that something wasn't right. Or maybe not. Maybe you believed your marriage was perfect and this is the biggest shock in your life.

Everything around you has changed. The things you live with; the schedule you kept; if you moved as a result of the divorce there is nothing around you to ground you and remind you of safer and easier times. The things you did together and the places you went are reminders of the loss of the marriage. Those memories, instead of providing you with a sense of peace and happiness, are like nightmares. You may be avoiding certain places or people because they remind you too much of happier times. You may feel your life getting smaller and smaller. The connections you made to a meaningful life are slipping away.

Every morning you wake up feeling dread, anxiety, and depression. Sometimes you are unable to stop crying. Your fears – about how you are going to support yourself, if you will ever love again, or, more importantly, if anyone will ever love you – haunt you day and night.

There are days that you are so filled with anger and rage that you secretly plot revenge or imagine horrible things happening to your ex. These visions are so startling to you, because they are so *not* you that they fill you with fear or more sadness. Your friends and family add to this with their negative or hateful comments. If they are trying to help, why does it hurt so much?

Are you sleeping through the night? Probably not. Or maybe you are sleeping all the time. Are you eating regularly? Probably not. Have you gained or lost weight suddenly? Does your body hurt in unexpected ways? Do you have unexplainable symptoms? Does your brain feel foggy and unable to make decisions clearly? All of these are temporary. I bring them up to let you know that these things happen to many of us when we go through this shocking transition.

Do you wonder where God is in all this? You may not have had faith in God, but at this point, you may be wondering, if you did, where God is and if your faith was misguided in the first place.

Is your house messier than it has ever been or are you spending a lot of time organizing and cleaning it to stay busy? Do all the mementos of your marriage – all the things you bought together – cause you to feel like you've been punched in the stomach? What are you wearing? Do black and blue feel like the only colors available to you right now?

In moments of dreaming are you able to see a new you? A recovered you? A you who has what you want? A you who is a success and flourishing? This *will* happen for you. I will say that again. This *will* happen for you. You are in charge of making sure that it does. There is a process to recovery from any grievous loss, which a divorce usually is. It is not a clear-cut, one-step-after-the-other, type of process. Each of us goes through it differently. We follow the same steps, just in a different order. What may have been crucial for me to address first when I divorced may already be handled for you. Every aspect of your life and your identity bears looking at anew and with intention in order to rebuild a life that is joyously yours.

Before we move forward and identify what this book can help you with, I need to say something about what I call the "bad stuff." If bad stuff happened to you during your marriage, this book will not help you work it all out. By bad stuff, what I mean is abuse: verbal, physical, emotional, sexual, or any ways in which your boundaries were violated. To help with this, you will need a different kind of professional help, which I will describe a bit later in the book. I had to deal with some of this during my marriage and divorce. I wish I'd had this book to help me with the rest.

This, too, will pass, and pass easily. I've been where you are, and I found my way forward to healed and happy. So can you.

Chapter One
YOU ARE NOT ALONE

I saw her wince, I saw her cry
I saw the glory in her eye
Myself, I long for love and light,
but must it come so cruel, must it be so bright?
– Leonard Cohen, *Joan of Arc, Stranger Music*

When I stepped through the curtains of the dressing room at the bridal shop in Brooklyn, my bridesmaid, Deb, and my maid of honor, Sandy, spontaneously burst into tears. My dress was beautiful beyond imagining and it transformed me into the perfect, the quintessential bride. It didn't matter how much it cost. This was *my* dress. It fit my picture of my perfect marriage to my perfect husband, and would make sure that this perfection was sealed.

Now, I already knew that he was far from perfect. But marriage before my friends, family, and God, in a picturesque and quaint Connecticut church was going to iron out all the imperfections and bring us to what I thought of then as the ideal state of being: married to a handsome man and on the road to building a successful life together.

I did get that first part right. We found a wonderful little white church in a bucolic neighborhood in Connecticut. I had the dress of a princess, three gorgeous bridesmaids, and three handsome grooms. My youngest brother was my ring bearer in his little tuxedo. Both of our families attended, as did hundreds of our friends. The pastor told the story of the Velveteen Rabbit, encouraging us to know that love gets deeper as it gets raggedy and worn through the years. We cried and kissed. Our guests cried and hugged. Our wedding photo album is a treasure of beauty. In short, we created the perfect wedding!

We lasted for 14 years. In those years, we traveled the world together. We bought a cabin in upstate New York and then my dream home in California. He was my best friend, my companion, my advisor, my family, and for some years, my sole provider. A lot of the time, I thought I was living the dream.

But the cracks that had been there even when we were dating widened when we began living together and eventually became chasms during the marriage. What do you do when the road you dreamed of develops chasms? Well, of course, you get really, really good at building bridges. Or at catapulting over them. Or at finding a long path around to the other side. That's what I did. Instead of facing the cracks directly, we both figured out ways to avoid them, temporarily repair them, and keep moving on.

Before I describe some of the pressures that cracked and then destroyed my marriage, I have to say that there was absolutely no lack of love in my marriage. We did not divorce because we stopped loving each other, because we fell in love with someone else, or because we realized we never had loved each other. Love was not the issue. Not really.

My ex-husband was gay and didn't want to be. He thought and I bought into a reality where this could be ignored and wished away. He struggled with hating himself for his attraction to men. We spent lots of time in therapy, relationship workshops, and in other attempts to "process" the discord between us that was caused by this very simple fact. It speaks volumes about the depth of our denial of reality when I tell you that it took us 14 years to realize this was not going to work. This was not going to be the perfect, ideal union of a marriage that we both so desperately wanted. I wanted a fairy tale romance. He wanted to be heterosexual. Great fantasies, both of them.

My ex-husband died in 2016 saving someone else's life while swimming off the coast of Mexico. That is who he was. He gave a lot to a lot of people. Including me. And yet....

Our marriage was filled with incredibly ugly, drunken, violent scenes. Like the time he called from the freeway raging and clearly intoxicated. Driving home, he threatened me over the phone. I called my sister to come over. We were both waiting for him, hoping that her presence would calm him down. His car screeched into the driveway. He crashed into the garage door with a tremendous bang. Car door slamming. Steps pounding up to the front door. He flung the door open with such force that it cracked hard against the wall. His eyes were wide and bloodshot. His nostrils flared with his labored breath. He paused only momentarily in his trajectory when he saw my sister. He stepped forward and slammed her against the wall, screaming at her to, "Get out! Get out of my house!" She stayed with me while I gathered my things. We both left. I, for the weekend, to reconsider. My sister, for the duration of my marriage to him.

The regular threats, physical abuse, and rages followed by the next day's silent treatment were intermittent. They were followed by periods where he was conciliatory in profoundly moving ways. Not just with huge bouquets of roses delivered to my work, but trips to magical places, spa treatments, and fabulous jewelry. It was a wild, wild ride from the depths of rage and hatred to the heights of bliss and beauty. Through all of this, I continued to love him. Changing the gender in the Longfellow poem so it makes sense, I used to say that, "When he was good he was very, very good and when he was bad he was horrid." I convinced myself for 14 long years that the good made up for the horrid. Towards the end of the marriage, in an attempt to again catapult over the chasm, he flew me to Paris for Valentine's Day and ushered me into the most ornately stunning hotel room I had ever seen. Ten-foot-tall French windows opened out onto the sparkling night skyline of Paris. We had dinner in a basement restaurant off a cobbled street, where I imagined brilliant French artists had sat and eaten before me. The romance was palpable. He told me over a glass of delicious French wine that he wanted to "see other people." I put down my wine glass and said, "No, not if you want to stay married to me." We left our meals unfinished as I started to cry. We returned to the romantic hotel room. His anger escalated as he attempted to convince me of the reasonableness of his need. As I sat at an 18th century desk weeping, he strode over to face me, grabbed my face and shook it so hard that the next morning I had fingerprint shaped bruises on both of my cheeks. That was the night – Valentine's Day – that our marriage ended. It took until August to negotiate a divorce. In November, with six of my female friends helping me carry boxes and furniture, I moved out of our dream home in the pouring rain. My devoted friends made trip after trip up and down the dark, wet steps to load up our cars and take me to my new little yellow house. My tears flowed like the rain on the night streets.

When my friends left me in my new home with all my wet boxes and our cats, my own transition from married to divorced to single began. Let me be perfectly clear. I did not welcome it at all. I knew intellectually that there was no going back. There was no way to fix it, no possible bridge that could be built to reach across the chasm this time. Still I cried every night for a year about wanting my dream back. I wanted that picture of perfect love, life-long companionship and unconditional support that I had worked so feverishly to believe in.

My process involved slowly coming out of denial about what was and making peace with it. I tried a lot of things. Frankly, I wallowed in misery for too long before I reached out for help. I was broken, afraid, alone, ashamed, and hopeless. Some decisions I made were helpful. Some, not so much. I do believe that life only gives us love and/or lessons. At that time, I continued to get a lot more lessons, as I didn't know how to connect to the love. I muddled through for years. Which is the reason I have decided to write this book.

You don't have to muddle through. You don't have to take years to heal from the disappointment and devastation of losing your marriage. I am not saying it will be quick, easy, and overnight. What I am saying is that you can take advantage of the things I learned to guide you on your way. You don't have to make as many missteps as I did.

One of the gifts of my divorce was that I also got to use these lessons in my work with both my clients and the people who I train to be clinicians. I believe I got these lessons in order to become an effective teacher who can support women to find their way out of that dark, dark place and into the sunshine.

Chapter Two
THE PATH

Say not, "I have found the path of the soul."
Say rather, "I have met the soul walking on the path."
For the soul walks upon all paths.
The soul walks not upon a line, neither does
it grow like a reed.
The soul unfolds itself, like a lotus of countless petals.
– Khalil Gibran, *The Prophet*

I don't think I'm going too far out on a limb to guess that your divorce came with an onslaught of intense feelings and an overwhelming to-do list. Doesn't it feel unfair that at a time when all you want to do is crawl into bed – or even under it – there are suddenly a slew of tasks and details that need to be handled? What this book and I can help you with is to guide you through the recovery process, step-by-step.

In the coming pages, you will learn practices that you can use for life so that if your boat is ever rocked like it is now, you have ways to steady yourself. I don't want you to need this book again ten years from now. I know you don't either. One of the risks of not doing the work now is that you could find yourself in another relationship – even marriage – and repeat the same scenario over again. This is remarkably common. One of the reasons I wrote this book is to help you avoid that. No guarantees, but if you take the steps in this book and practice the practices, you are more likely to create a different result. Your future is in your hands. I am reaching out to hold them.

Chapter Three will help you understand the difference between a change and a transition. Chapters Four through Six will address some common areas that need immediate attention in your life such as money, housing, etc. I will give you practices to help with these areas. In Chapter Seven, you will begin to assess yourself and discover more deeply who you are now. Chapter Eight will teach some practices to deepen your connection to yourself and your spirituality. In Chapter Nine, we will start to look at marriage as a choice. Chapter Ten will focus on the lessons learned. Chapter Eleven will give you practices to support you in manifesting your new life. In Chapter Twelve, I will describe ways you could stay stuck or have difficulty moving forward as rapidly as you might want to. Finally, in Chapter Thirteen, you will create a new Life Plan to follow.

EXERCISE

We are starting out fun and easy. I want you to pull out your iPod, open up Pandora, and listen to upbeat, happy, inspiring music during the day. One song I recommend: *Three Little Birds* – Bob Marley.

Chapter Three
THE TRANSITION

*Nothing is so painful to the human mind as a
great and sudden change.*
– Mary Wollstonecraft Shelley, *Frankenstein*

There is a model for understanding how to move from an actual change in your life through to a new understanding of it. This is called The Transition Framework. It was created by William Bridges for the purpose of helping companies, teams, and individuals adapt to change and honor the emotional component that comes with these changes. So why am I referencing a corporate model for change in a book about being newly divorced?

We throw the words change and transition around like they are interchangeable. Mr. Bridges teaches that they are not. For you, one change happened on the day you got divorced. There may also be a series of changes that happened related to that. Each of them is an event with a date on the calendar. We can't do much about them. They happened. What we are going to talk about is how you are dealing, coping, and making decisions around each of them. These are your transitions – the emotional responses to the changes you have gone through. Each change brings with it a corresponding transition.

Your path changed direction when you got divorced. We are going to examine where you are on your path. The reason to do this is to see what it will take, and to do what it will take, to nurture the transition from the state of being married through the state of being divorced. It is also my goal to help you to accept joyfully being single again. This transition is from one identity to another. It is from one status to another. Each identity and/or status had or has its own set of meanings and values for you. For instance, being married means something to you that is different from what it means to me. Being single or divorced also has an individualized meaning to you. Let's look at that now.

Your exercises in this chapter involve journaling, so if you have one, please pull it out now.

 ## EXERCISE

Buy yourself a beautiful journal. The one that jumps off the shelf at the bookstore. The one you can't stop looking at. It doesn't matter if it is lined, unlined, big, or small. Just buy it.

Get some colorful pens that you love writing with. I love multi-color gel pens because they write so smoothly. Maybe you love writing with a fountain pen.

(Optional) Get some fun stickers from the local craft store to decorate the pages of your journal as you write. Flowers, cartoon characters, stars, whatever floats your boat.

Here are some questions to answer in your journal:

- ✓ What did it mean to you to be married?
- ✓ How did it make you feel about yourself to call yourself someone's wife?
- ✓ What does it mean to you to have a husband?
- ✓ What did it mean to you to be a married couple?
- ✓ When you were out in the world as a married woman, whether with your husband or without him, how was that different from how it is today to be out in the world knowing you are divorced?

Now let's dig a little deeper. Again, write your answers to these in your journal.

- ✓ What are some things that you did to let everyone know that you were married? Of course there are the obvious things like wearing a wedding ring. But what else?
- ✓ Did you just happen to mention in conversation with a new person the words "my husband" in order to let them know your marital status?
- ✓ When talking about future plans, did you always say "we" instead of "I?"
- ✓ Was your husband often the main character in the stories you told to friends and family?

✓ Did your stories illustrate the ways in which you were together, the fun you had, or the ways you knew each other?

✓ Maybe your stories to friends weren't always about the happiness in being married but were about the struggles, conflicts, and challenges. How did you talk about your marriage with others? How often?

The answers to these questions should begin to inform you about your identity as a married person. There is absolutely nothing bad or wrong about any of this. There is nothing to feel embarrassed about or to wonder if you should have done differently. Please *do not* go there! You are black and blue enough without beating yourself up.

The stories we tell ourselves and others define us. They define our identities and how we fit into the social world. They provide clues on how to interact with each other. This is why we do it. Telling the handsome, young man at the gym that your husband has a personal trainer lets him know that you are not available. But thanks for flirting with me anyway.

We are defining the ways in which you established and maintained your identity as a married person. The shifting and transforming of this identity started with the change of the divorce. This transition comes with its own set of emotions. When your identity was one of being married, you may have felt pride, a sense of belonging, and thought that you were doing things right. Alternately, you may have felt trapped and confused as you sensed there was something wrong in the marriage. Either way, you still identified as married. Either happily or not. The identity from being a married person is the transition we have to make.

Now you are in uncharted waters. Not married. Not single. You are divorced. What does that mean anyway? I will talk about that in detail in Chapter Nine, The Choice. For now, what we're going to do is look at how you are moving away from the status and identity of being married. I know firsthand how crummy and confusing that moving away feels.

Your marriage ended. That is the change. The meaning you give that statement is at the heart of many of your emotions right now. When something ends, we often feel loss and grief. But not always. You lost something when your marriage ended. You may or may not have wanted to lose it.

Did your divorce bring other changes to your life? Did you move; start or end a job; stop wearing your wedding ring; buy a new bed; get a new car; take public transportation instead of driving; or drive yourself instead of your husband doing it? Each of these represents a change as well as a loss. How you feel about each of those things is going to be different and part of the path you will take into a new identity.

For instance, when I took off my wedding ring, I also removed the watch and another ring he had given me on different anniversaries. I put them in my jewelry box with feelings of elation and freedom. I felt like I was taking off handcuffs. I couldn't get them off fast enough. Those feelings lasted for months until one day I opened my jewelry box, saw the beautiful rings, and felt such remorse and sadness.

When I started driving myself everywhere, I experienced a lot of road rage. I hate driving. My ex-husband had done the

driving when we were together. I got to be good as a navigator, in the days before we all had GPS. I enjoyed this role and
gave good directions. When I had to start doing all my own
driving, I was not happy. I was also nervous since I didn't
have a navigator. I finally got good at using my GPS so it got
easier. Today, I still don't like driving much but feel confident,
secure, and good about my abilities. I've also, thankfully,
learned to manage my road rage.

I didn't buy a new bed but took ours with me when I moved.
If you did buy a new bed, you may have ambivalent feelings
when you sleep in it for the first time. You may feel lonely
and sad to not have his body in the bed next to you. I sure did.
At the same time, you may love having all that space in the
bed and to be able to sleep on either side wherever you want.
Yup, really liked that part. Mostly for me, I loved not have his
snoring wake me up in the middle of the night. But you may
miss it.

Each of the things that changed as a result of your divorce
will bring its own set of feelings and its own timeline for
resolving these feelings. They will be your feelings and won't
be the same as other people who have gone through the same
changes. It is messy. Some things you will adapt to quickly,
easily, and they won't be a big deal. Others may take time. If
you use the practices I am going to teach you in this book, they
will help you to move through them. You may slip and slide
back and forth between feeling good and feeling not so good
about some of them.

It's all good. My goal is to help you recognize all the things
that have changed alongside your marital status and give you
the tools and practices to move you along your path in a grace-
ful and steady way.

EXERCISE

In your new, beautiful journal make a list of the things you believe you lost as a result of the marriage ending.

Naming some of these may make you sad, cry, or get really angry. Naming others may make you feel relief or even excitement.

After you complete your list, take a look back at it.

Now write a one word feeling next to each thing that you lost.

An example from mine:

The watch he gave me for our fifth anniversary – relief

My gorgeous house on the hill – terrible sadness

Each and every one of those feelings is legitimate. Please do not judge them. It is equally important not to compare yourself to other divorced people. Especially if they have been divorced for longer than you have. Just because your friend was able to say, "Good riddance to bad rubbish," when she donated her wedding dress to the Salvation Army, does not mean that you are wrong for wanting to keep yours or for crying when you look at it.

I wanted you to examine the losses you have experienced in order to begin both the healing and the reconstitution of yourself in the next chapters. Take a moment to appreciate that despite these losses, you are still here, still standing!

(Optional exercise: Listen to a piece of music that never fails to move you. *Canon in D Major* by Johann Pachelbel always works for me, no matter who plays it.)

Chapter Four

WHAT DO I DO
ABOUT...??

A straight line exists between me and the good things.
I have found the line and its direction is known to me.
Absolute trust keeps me going in the right direction.
Any intrusion is met with a heart full of the good thing.
– Talking Heads, *The Good Thing*

There are areas of your life that need attention right now. As we saw in the last chapter, some things have changed. Some things may need to change even further. Here, I am going to help you look at some of the practical areas of your life and begin to think about what you might do differently, either more of, or less of. Let's talk about your job or career; the state of your finances; what to do about dating; your health; and your physical presentation. We are going to start with your health and physical presentation because it is hard to make any headway in the other areas when we aren't taking care of ourselves. Get out that trusty journal and prepare to take notes. We will look at each issue individually. I will give you exercises to do related to each. If you choose to do them, they will help you to move through these issues more fluidly.

Your Body, Your Self

Your Health

On a scale from 1 – 10, with 1 being the worst ever and 10 being optimal, radiant health, how would you rate your current health? Write the number down in your journal like this: My current health is a 4.

If you rated yourself anything lower than a 6, I want you to put down this book, pick up the phone and make an appointment with your doctor(s). If it is after hours, leave a message. Why? Because you have undergone a big stressor. Divorce. Stress has a direct impact on our immune systems. Check this out:

Ongoing stress makes us susceptible to illness and disease because the brain sends defense signals to the endocrine system, which then releases an array of hormones that not only gets us ready for emergency situations but severely depresses our immunity at the same time. Some experts claim that stress is responsible for as much as 90% of all illnesses and diseases, including cancer and heart disease.

– Andrew Goliszek, *Ph.D., Psychology Today*

Sounds pretty bad, huh? I'm not predicting major health issues for you. It is a good idea to get yourself checked out to see what your current baseline is. If you have any serious or ongoing medical issues, please follow up with your doctor(s) to make sure the conditions are staying steady. Many of the practices in this book support decreasing your stress, and at the same time, improving your health, both mental and, in this case, physical.

I assisted one of my clients, Joan, when she exclaimed in the middle of a session, "My shoulder is killing me!" I guided her in a dialog with her shoulder, asking, "What does your shoulder want to say to you right now?" Her shoulder had some choice four letter words to say about not feeling that she was taking care of herself. We did a back and forth dialog with her shoulder for a few minutes. She had an "Aha!" moment when she realized what was causing it. When I checked in with her the following week, it no longer hurt. Relief from our stress-related ailments can be quite simple. We do have to seek it, however.

I am going to introduce you to a lot of what I call "practices" in this book. What I mean is something that we choose to do regularly and habitually. We may not be all that good at doing it initially. The practice part – the doing it over and over on a regular basis – makes us better at it and integrates it into our lives. Meditation and yoga are common examples of practices. You do them regularly and you get certain positive results. Journaling is a practice.

This book is for you to use as it suits you. Take what you like, in terms of which practices to make a regular part of your life, and leave the rest. I do suggest that you try each of them before deciding they are not for you. If you want things to change, you have to do something about it. Practicing is doing.

Okay, back to your health. When you meet with your doctor(s), make sure to tell them that you have recently divorced and about whatever other changes you have gone through. If your doctor doesn't get it immediately that this is important information for your overall health, sorry, but I think you need a new doctor. If your doctor has prescriptions for you, whether medical or things like "get more exercise," think seriously about doing them. You can choose not to do them, but take some time to discern if they would be helpful to you.

Some of the practices I teach will be helpful for healing from what I called the "bad stuff." They help restore your sense of yourself. If you are experiencing any of the following symptoms, I would advise finding a therapist and even a psychiatrist for a trial of medication. Symptoms of traumatic stress from abuse include but are not limited to: feeling suicidal or homicidal, hyper-vigilance, relentless depression, nightmares, panic attacks, extreme anxiety, disassociation, an exaggerated startle response, avoiding places or people that remind you of the bad stuff, and recurring experiences as if they are happening again.

A psychiatrist usually only prescribes psychotropic medications to treat your symptoms of depression or anxiety. If you see one and they do prescribe medication for you, I recommend Googling the medication before you fill the prescription. Many come with side effects, which you should know about. Many take a while to work. Sometimes it takes a few trials to find the right one. Make sure to get all of your questions answered either by the psychiatrist or online. Don't worry that you need to be on them for life. They treat symptoms not the "disease." As you find ways to heal the "dis-ease," your symptoms could diminish.

Finding a therapist is a little bit like finding a cross between a new partner and a best friend. Because you are paying them, you don't have to do anything to make the relationship work except show up. Your therapist should be a person who you would trust and whose judgment you would seek. They should be at least as intelligent as you are. You may not like them all the time. That's okay and actually to be expected. You should be able to tell them about it when you are mad at them; they have hurt your feelings or misunderstood you. Keep in mind that many therapies that are effective in working with traumatic stress or abuse are nonverbal therapies, not traditional talk therapy. These involve art, music, movement, horses, yoga, and other activities besides talking.

I am licensed as a therapist, but in these pages I am acting as a Life Coach for you. I will be directive and focused on helping you in your personal development and life choices. I will not, as a therapist, offer treatment for any mental health issues such as depression and anxiety.

Back to your health.

 EXERCISE

Watch a three-minute video on YouTube by Prince Ea, *A Message from Your Body.* After you watch it, use your journal and make yourself a list of all the things you thought of that you are doing now that are impacting your body.

- ✓ How are you eating and what?
- ✓ Are you sleeping through the night?
- ✓ How much are you drinking and what?
- ✓ Do you smoke?
- ✓ What are you doing for exercise and physical activity?
- ✓ How are you taking care of your body or how are you neglecting it?

Tell the truth to yourself. Leave the guilt and shame out of it.

You can use this list to see where you want to start to make changes.

We like to say to follow the Golden Rule and treat others the way we like to be treated. This starts with ourselves. Are you treating yourself how you like to be treated? Many of the Twelve Step Recovery programs recommend using the acronym HALT to help manage stress. People who struggle with addictions are often triggered by stress to use whatever their substance of choice is (food, alcohol, cigarettes, gambling, etc.). Here's what HALT stands for and how to use it.

H = Hungry
A = Angry (I add Anxious here, too)
L = Lonely
T = Tired

The practice of HALT is to first, notice when you are feeling stressed. Then, immediately check in with yourself and ask yourself, "Am I hungry? Angry or anxious? Lonely? or Tired?" When I am most stressed, I'm usually a combination of several of them like, hungry, tired, and angry. Once you figure out which one or ones are affecting you, the practice of using HALT is to do something about it right away. Hungry? Get a snack. Drink some water, too. Lonely? Pick up the phone and call someone just to say, "Hi." Angry or anxious? Vent about those feelings to the person you called. You might notice that your feelings change most easily by doing something physical, like taking a walk around the block or dancing to some loud music. Move that body to move those feelings! Tired? Take a break. If you can't take a nap or lie down, just take a little stretch break and acknowledge that you are tired. Make a plan to take care of it. Go to bed early that night or sleep late the next morning.

When I acknowledge to myself and my body that I feel any of these, it truly helps. The acknowledgment moves me into problem-solving mode where I am in charge – as opposed to feeling at the effect of my stress and irritability.

Your Presentation

What about your physical presentation? I'm going to use the example of a car. In the above section, you had your systems checked by your mechanic (i.e., the doctor) and got recommendations for what to do to make it run better and last longer. Now, let's look at how it looks. Is it clean and shiny on the outside or covered with bird poop and spider webs? When was the last time the seats were vacuumed? The windows washed? In California, where I live, people judge each other by the model of their cars and how they keep them looking. I don't put a lot of stock in this but have had people get annoyed with me when my car hadn't been washed recently enough. They didn't want to ride in it.

What about you? Not your car, although if the analogy applies there, too, it's worth considering. Are you getting up each day and facing it all clean and shiny? Are you having a hard time getting out of the same pajamas you've been wearing for a week? When was the last time you got your hair cut? Are you wearing makeup, if you usually do, or have you given that up for now?

We can head in one or two directions in the early stages of adapting to divorce. Some of us put on the armor. We dress up perfectly. Do the makeup flawlessly. Take care of our presentation perfectly because God forbid that someone might notice that we are falling apart inside. Or even that we are hurting.

Some of us allow the falling apart to show. We show up in all black, rumpled clothing with no make-up and unwashed hair. We might not even leave the house because we look like such a mess.

This is on a continuum. You may fall anywhere between these two poles. Let's say you are in the first group. You are making sure that you look perfect, so no one will notice that anything is different about you. My advice to you is to keep doing it. You are doing what we call "acting as if." You are acting as if things are the same. They aren't, but this gives your body and the Universe the message that you've got this. You can handle this. At the same time, you must take care of the hurt girl inside to make sure her needs are getting met. You don't want the temporary armor to turn into permanent armor. When that happens, we put up walls that keep connection at bay and slow or halt our own healing. Think about the character Meryl Streep played in *The Devil Wears Prada*. Do you want to become her? Maybe you do. She had great clothing! She also had a broken and brittle heart.

If you are in the second group and you can't deal with the thought of trying to put yourself together, I've got some bad news for you. You need to do it. But it's okay to be gentle and loving with yourself. You are hurting, wounded, and recovering. Just like you rarely see people in the hospital with their hair and makeup done wearing their nicest outfits, it is okay to spend some time in your PJs, robe and with messy hair. What I don't want is for you to get stuck there. This is where the seeds of depression hang out. My suggestion, if this is you, is to go online and buy yourself some pretty new PJs that make you feel yummy, comforted, and even sexy. Put clean sheets on your bed. Luxuriate in them. Entice your senses with nice feeling, smelling, and looking things to pull you back into the world of wanting to look your greatest.

Now let's move on to talking about what to do about dating.

Dating: Just Don't Do It!

In the movie 28 Days with Sandra Bullock, there is a scene where a newly recovered addict who wants an intimate relationship is given the advice to first get a green plant. Keep the plant alive for a year. If you can do that, you can graduate to a pet. If you can keep the pet alive for a year, then you can start to think about dating and a relationship with a partner.

I am not saying that recovering from divorce is the same as recovering from an addiction, but there are some words of wisdom here. They gave this advice to the addicts to help them learn to care about others, instead of being so narcissistically focused on themselves. When you are newly divorced, you *need* to be narcissistically focused on yourself. That means you can forget about getting the plant or the pet but that you should, in most instances, forgo any real thought about jumping into a new relationship right away.

I bet you know people who did. There are those people who met their "soul mates" right after they got divorced and have been happy ever since. If you are one of them, God bless and keep you. I am waiting for the other shoe to drop. That may be my cynicism showing through.

It is okay to go window shopping. It's great fun to look at online dating sites to see who is out there. It can be inspiring, funny, and a turn on. It can also be kind of grim. Either way, I would say that it's fine to look, but don't touch. Don't start casting your net out to find the new husband, partner, or replacement. Your wounded heart needs time to heal. Allowing someone in too soon is liable to leave both of you more injured and bloody.

What is common, and I bet you can think of someone who did this, is to find a replica of your ex and get involved with them. They may not look like them, although often they do. Usually the same issues; same problems; and the same barriers to intimacy show up. We can't see them right off due to the flush of hormonal blindness that is caused by being in lust. When they do show up, they are the brutal demise of what seemed like a fresh start.

Here's a mistake I almost made. Several months after my divorce, I went to an evening of spiritual music with a girlfriend. We were there to hear a famous performer who performed chants in Sanskrit. Another man began the concert by playing the harmonium and chanting a song that we knew. As we sang along with him, I noticed how beautiful he was. His singing was deeply touching, and I was drawn to his energy. I imagined him to be kind, generous, and loving based on how he was performing. I felt myself wanting him. After the concert was over, I sought him out and, to the best of my ability, flirted with him. I should say that I'm not a very good flirt. Pretty clumsy at it, actually. In any case, he got that I was attempting to flirt with him. He was kind, gentle, and direct when he looked in my eyes and said, "I am a monk, you know." Meaning, of course, that he was celibate by choice. I thanked him for his music and walked away, somewhat embarrassed. Instead of being attracted to a man who could not find me sexually interesting because I was a woman, like my ex, I was now attracted to one who had renounced sex as part of his spiritual path. I was batting 1000 here! It got even worse. As my girlfriend and I walked back to the car, we shared how moving the evening was. She, who had not witnessed my flirtation and rejection by the monk, said, apropos of nothing, "Did you notice that the monk who played first looked just like your ex?" I was dumbfounded. I literally stopped dead in the street. "He did?" I asked with astonishment. "Yes," she said. "He looked exactly like him except not so angry. Like a kinder and gentler version of him." I truly had not seen this at all.

So, as far as dating goes, do me a favor and do the opposite of the Nike slogan: Just Don't Do It! Yet.

You have some healing to do and a new identity to form. Let's make sure that you know who the *you* is who is going to get into a new relationship before you begin to date.

I believe that there are lots of lessons you have learned, are beginning to learn, or will learn through the process of reading this book. These lessons will help you to create a successful and lasting connection in the future if that is what you want. Be patient, dear heart!

Money and Work

Figuring out what to do about money and work at this juncture is a completely individual issue. I can only point you in some general directions since I don't know the specifics of your situation. If I were working with you as your life coach, we would make a very detailed plan that spoke directly to what is needed in this area of your life. To make this plan on your own, I can start you off with questions to ask yourself, some ideas, and suggestions.

When I was going through the process of divorcing, I was not working. Quickly, I realized that I needed to go back to work. It was not a huge challenge to find a position. My emotional state was so erratic, however, that I knew that I would not be able to show up as the professional I knew I could be. During the hiring conversation, I disclosed to my soon-to-be supervisor that I was going through a divorce; that I knew I was not at my best; and that I was committed to learning the new position quickly. I told him that I wanted him to know that while my work may not start out as the best I can bring that I was committed to getting there. This type of candid conversation may or may not serve you, depending on your potential work place. I would ask you to consider though, if your place of work and your direct supervisor does not support you in a meaningful way when you are in one of the biggest transitions of your life, is this the right place and the right people with whom to spend a majority of your waking hours?

This is the time for you to re-evaluate what is important to you; what gifts you have to bring; and who you want to grow into being. Like an uprooted plant needs tender care, water, and good soil to put down new roots and continue to grow, so do you. Give yourself that in making a choice of what to do about your work life.

Managing your money and investments and figuring out your retirement plan may be overwhelming. Maybe you have that totally handled. If you do, high five!! Keep doing what you are doing. If it is adding stress to your life, I recommend finding a good financial advisor. Many of them will initially consult with you for free in order to allow you to understand what they have to offer. My next door neighbor was a financial advisor. He has been a mainstay in helping me figure out my financial needs and how to get them met.

If fears of homelessness and scarcity begin to haunt your thoughts and play through your mind during the day and sleepless nights, we need to start changing them. Our fears can condition us to invite into our lives exactly the things we are the most afraid of.

*I learned that courage was not the absence of
fear, but the triumph over it.
The brave man is not he who does not feel
afraid, but he who conquers that fear.*

– Nelson Mandela

How do we conquer our fears? One at a time. One step at a time. One thought at a time. The practices we will explore in the next chapter will not only help to alleviate fear but will help to move you into a state of receptivity so that financial prosperity has a way to find you.

 EXERCISE

On a piece of loose writing paper this time, not your journal, write a letter to your future self. Describe what your life is like in your ideal future. How do you look? How are you dressed? Where do you live? What do you like about it? Describe in as much detail as you can all aspects of your life. Don't worry about the writing style. Paint a picture with words to let yourself see your future. What does your bank account look like? Your home? Be as detailed as possible. Be kind and expansive in your language.

My letter might start out, "Dear Marsha, I see you have moved into the house by the sea that you always wanted. I love the expansive deck looking out over the beach, where you spend your afternoons watching the dolphins and whales. I am so happy that you are surround-ing yourself with the things that give you the most joy, like your two little dogs, your vegetable garden, and that amazing library full of interesting books...."

When you finish your letter put it in an envelope and address it to yourself. Put a date six months from now in the upper right corner where a stamp would go. Put it in a safe place. Mark your calendar for that date. Come back and read it in six months.

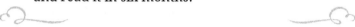

I hope you are taking the time to complete the exercises so far. They can increase the speed and ease with which you recover your sense of yourself and your confidence. If you have questions or want additional support, please contact me at marsha@marshavaughn.com.

Chapter Five

JUMPSTARTING YOUR JOY

Joy is the best makeup.
– Anne Lamott, *Grace*

L et's look at how to come to life again from the inside out. In the previous chapter, we saw areas of your life where you could make concrete, tangible, and measureable external changes, like in what you are wearing. Here are some practices that can start the process of internal change. If you are familiar with them and use them every day, congratulations! Now might be the time to up your practice and as they say in Buddhism, "Practice like your hair is on fire."

We are going to look at three practices in this chapter – mindfulness, gratitude, and prayer – that can assist you in jumpstarting your joy. When I was transitioning from married to divorced to single, the idea of joy – the very concept, let alone the feeling – was a foreign one to me. "Joy??!! What is that?" I wondered every time I heard someone express that they felt it. I couldn't even identify it. Relief from pain and suffering was good enough for me. A momentary lift in my sadness felt like enough. But joy? Really?! I couldn't see it as a possibility. I started to look for it. I got curious about it. Could it be real? Was it a possibility for me? I wasn't sure how or what to do to find out. Mindfulness was one of my first steps on this road.

Mindfulness

In my post-divorce state, there were moments that were more than just a relief from the grimness. I didn't know to call them joy. They just felt like bright moments in an otherwise gray world. Sometimes these moments involved birds or flowers, both of which I love. I would be gloomily sitting outside, thinking about all of my losses and letting the waves of grief wash over me. At one of those bleak times, a little brown California towhee flew by and perched on a branch, eyeing me with her sparkly little eye. She jumped to the ground near me and began pecking and scratching in the garden soil, every so often looking up at me with mild interest. I watched her going about her birdy business and watched her watching me. We noticed each other in a neutral and non-threatening way. This was our conversation.

Towhee, "I see you."

Marsha, "I see you, too."

A few minutes later, she flew over my head and away to some other garden. I noticed immediately that I felt lighter, had a new sense of peace, and my grief was gone.

This is an example of mindfulness. Mindfulness is a practice where you just notice what you are doing, where you are, with complete attention. In this example, my complete and utter attention was with the towhee and no longer on my grim thoughts.

You can practice it doing anytime and anywhere, which is why it is great as a way to bring peace and joy into our lives.

Thich Nhat Hahn, the Vietnamese Buddhist teacher, teaches mindful walking. You can choose anything you do and choose to put your attention on it, as I did with watching the bird. For instance, you can wash your face, brush your teeth, make your bed, or even take out the trash in a mindful manner.

All it takes is to focus your complete attention on the task at hand. If you are washing your face, for instance, notice the temperature of the water and how it feels on your hands and face. Notice what your cheeks feel like. Does the water have a particular scent or smell? The skill involved in practicing mindfulness is the skill of noticing. Notice the tiny details about any activity and you are beginning to practice being mindful. Every time you practice it, it becomes more a part of what you do. Each time you notice the texture of the banana you are eating, the way it smells, and how the skin feels in your hand, you are practicing mindfulness.

It isn't necessary to make it a chore. You don't need to say to yourself, "Okay, now I'm going to practice mindfulness" and force yourself to do it. This is a gentle practice that involves a quality of allowing yourself to notice – in a moment-by-moment way – what you are doing. If it feels totally unfamiliar to you, you can certainly give yourself an assignment. You can pick a piece of fruit that you enjoy and give yourself the task of eating it mindfully. That will mean: not looking at your phone, not reading, not talking, or distracting yourself in any other way from the simple act of eating the piece of fruit. This can be challenging. The things we distract ourselves with call to us to pay attention to them. Our phones make chirping, beeping, and buzzing sounds to get our attention. You may need to put your phone on silent in order to eat a piece of fruit in peace with mindful attention.

I am recommending the practice of mindfulness to you now, at this juncture in your recovery from divorce, to help you to focus on this moment and this moment only. This moment where you will notice that things are okay. This moment where nothing bad and painful is actually happening to you. This moment where you are just eating a piece of fruit. As we string together moments of mindfulness, we begin to see that more and more of our day is okay and not painful. We open the door to peace and even to joy.

My towhee interaction and many others that followed during other dark times in my life, caused me to recognize birds as harbingers of peace and joy. When a little sparrow or mockingbird shows up and I am full of my discontent or a current stressor is marauding through my mind relentlessly, I know now to focus on the bird. The negativity just goes. I'm not even talking about hummingbirds here, who are, in my opinion, joy delivery birds. When one of these little blessing birds shows up, gratitude bursts forth in me.

Gratitude

You may not believe that you have anything to be grateful for at this moment in your life. In fact, you may feel so resentful and angry at the losses you have endured that the very word may make you want to throw the book across the room. Go ahead and throw it, if you want. Then come back and let's talk about how to get there and, more importantly, why.

Gratitude is a powerful mood-altering practice. It has the magical power to alter your moods and the power to alter your external reality. Gratitude is the spark that creates the possibility for manifesting all of our dreams, desires, and good stuff. When we express gratitude, it is like a magnet for more of what we are grateful for to enter our lives. I love to play with gratitude to watch this happen.

One way I did this recently was to say, "Thank you!" every time I found a penny on the street. I picked up the penny, brought it home, and put it in a special cup. I did this each time I found a penny. In a couple of weeks, I noticed that I could rarely leave the house without finding a penny or more. On one walk, the sidewalk was littered with them. I use this as a simple example of how gratitude can assist you in attracting good to you. It is an easy place to start if you doubt your own abilities to manifest. There are pennies everywhere!

A woman I work with shared that she was completely burnt out from her work; hated everything about her job, her coworkers, and her life. I listened to her release all of this venom. I, in effect, held the garbage bag out while she filled it up. Then I guided her gently to what she was grateful for about the exact things that she had hated. Her eyes welled with tears when she spewed hatred. When she was able to switch to gratitude, her shoulders relaxed, her eyes brightened, and in a few moments a large smile crossed her face. The situation had not changed, but her experience of it had switched dramatically.

 EXERCISE

Let's try this. Take out your journal.

Rate your current mood on a scale from 1 – 10. If you are irritable, 1 means that you are not irritable at all. 10 means that you want to throat punch someone. If you are sad, 1 is just okay. 10 is you can't stop crying. Put the number at the top of the page.

Under the number, make a list of all of the things you are grateful for today. Put them in a sentence using this form, "I am grateful for...." If you are having difficulty coming up with a list, here is a cheat sheet:

✓ I am grateful I am alive.

✓ I am grateful for my health.

✓ I am grateful I have a roof over my head.

✓ I am grateful I have food to eat today.

✓ I am grateful I can read.

✓ I am grateful for flowers.

✓ I am grateful for my dog/cat/gerbil/ snake, etc.

✓ I am grateful for my job.

✓ I am grateful for my blue sweater (or other favorite piece of clothing).

✓ I am grateful for running water and flush toilets.

✓ I am grateful for my family/friends.

✓ I am grateful to have a working car.

Keep going until you run out of things to be grateful for. Now, measure that irritability or sadness again. What number did you get to now? I bet the number came down. Your sadness may not have decreased, but you may feel a new sense of hopefulness that wasn't there before you made your list.

I find gratitude is an amazing practice to pull out and use when I feel especially victimized by something that has happened in my life. If I am angry at my boss, annoyed with someone who just cut me off in traffic, or hurt that a friend didn't respond the way I wanted them to, I pull out the gratitude. For example, noticing that I am angry at the jerk who just cut me off in traffic and endangered my life, I begin by saying, "I am grateful that my car works; that I have great brakes; that the sun is shining; and that the clouds are so beautiful…." I keep making a list, out loud if possible, until my feelings about being victimized are relieved.

This can be an advanced practice when you use it in the moment toward the person you believe has victimized you in some way. It works. It is a good idea to start first with the mundane things in life that you are grateful for and not jump right into being grateful for the bad driver. Just recite the list. After you feel your annoyance start to lift, you may find you can actually say the words, "I am grateful for that bad driver as he caused me to slow down," and mean it. It may feel begrudging at first. That is okay. Say it until your resentment has loosened up a bit.

Gratitude, when practiced regularly, increases our ability to be generous towards others. Being generous towards others increases our ability to be forgiving. They add together to increase our sense of peace and build up a storehouse of joy. There is no downside, so give it a try today.

Prayer

Prayer and meditation are two sides of a coin. I purposefully am not teaching you about sitting meditation in this book as there are many, many other meditation teachers who

do a brilliant job of it. Personally, I recommend Pema Chodron. The mindfulness practices discussed above are forms
of meditation.

It is said that prayer is when we talk to God. Meditation is
when we listen. If the word "God" doesn't resonate with you,
please feel free to substitute anything else that represents
something higher than our human existence: the Universe,
Nature, Being. Whatever word makes sense to you. I am
going to continue with "God" and/or "the Universe" because
that is what I call It.

When we pray, we are sending our words out into the Universe to God's ears. Our words have the power to manifest
anything and everything. That said, most of the words we send
out are unconscious in the form of repetitive thoughts. We
think all day long, sending out messages like a non-stop AM
radio station, which God hears. If I am thinking all through
the day, "I'm so miserable. No one will ever love me again," I
may think I am just expressing my low feelings. The bad news
is that I am broadcasting that to the Universe as a demand. I
am straight up telling God, "No one will ever love me again!!
Make sure that this is true!" All of our "woe is me" talk is an
actual demand, which we reinforce over and over, each time
we say or think these things.

Reverend Eloise Oliver, the Pastor of the East Bay Church
of Religious Science, teaches to "Pray without ceasing." If
you are facing a challenging time and ask her, "Oh, Reverend
E, what do I do about…?" Her answer is always the same.
After a pause, she says, "Pray on it."

If you have a way of praying that works for you, my advice
is to make sure you are doing it. Daily, throughout the day,
and definitely before falling asleep at night, say your prayers.

Prayer is talking to God. We have also been taught that it is asking for something. "Please don't let my cat die!" or "Please, God, if you give me this job, I promise to...." Maybe that type of prayer works for you. It hasn't been all that effective for me. I am only willing to teach what I know works so the prayer practices I am going to share, I have tested and experimented with. They work!

If you don't have a prayer practice, the gratitude practice we described is actually a prayer. You can just say, "Thank You!" as you go through your day. You got the parking spot in front of the store. Say, "Thank You!" You found the car keys after searching half an hour. Say, "Thank You!" You took the dog to the vet for a foxtail in his ear, and not only did he not have one, but they only charged you $50. Say, "Thank You!" Every penny you find on the street, say, "Thank You!"

"Thank You!" is the easiest prayer there is. Easy to remember and easy to do. I recommend using it with the people in your life. Someone holds the door for you as you are coming out behind them, say, "Thank You!" Say it to the person who packs your groceries; the person who takes money at the toll station; the person driving the sanitation truck and dealing with your garbage. Saying, "Thank You!" throughout the day will keep you in a place of gratitude and prayer.

If, rather than simply sending out your gratitude and a flurry of "Thank Yous!" you want to be more specific, you absolutely can. You don't want it to sound like you are beseeching a Higher Power to do your bidding, however. What most often works is when we get absolutely 100% clear in our entire being about our intention and put that into words. Here is an example from my own divorce.

My biggest fear, especially since I was not working at the time we decided to divorce, was that I would become homeless. It was not a completely rational fear as I did have family and friends who would have let me couch surf until I got on my feet. Nonetheless, I was terrified of it. My state of mind was panicked for most of my waking hours. When I am panicked, I don't make the clearest decisions or accomplish much of anything productive.

One day I visited my friend, Margo, who owned her own little house. I cried and railed about my ex-husband and my fears of being homeless. She listened with great empathy. She encouraged me by saying, "Hey, I was able to buy my house. If I can do it, you can." We stood on her porch looking across the street and I said with great passion, pointing at the little yellow house directly across from Margo's, "I want a house like that!"

The couple in that yellow house had just moved in a year ago and were in the process of doing renovations and designing their garden. I left Margo's and drove to the top of the Albany Hill. This hill has an open area on top, surrounded by towering eucalyptus trees and no houses. I stood in the clearing, tears streaming down my face and yelled into the sky, "God! I just want a home! I want a home like that little yellow house! Is that too much to ask?!" I am pretty sure that I used the F-bomb and all kinds of language. This was not a pious prayer. I yelled until I was done and had no more to say. I let it go and drove home.

A week later, Margo called me to tell me that the couple who owned the yellow house were divorcing and selling their house. I called my realtor immediately. We started the home buying process. I wrote the couple a letter telling them who I was and why I wanted their house. The real estate market in the San Francisco Bay Area was in one of its "heating up" phases. Realtors were licking their chops because every house that went up for sale had ten or more buyers bidding for it. Bidding wars, they were called. I entered the bidding war, knowing I didn't have the money that some of the other buyers had. I entered it knowing that I wanted to be Margo's neighbor and that this was my house. I envisioned myself there.

The night that the offers were being reviewed by the seller, I sat numb and spaced out with anxiety. After some prayer work, I was able to surrender and remind myself to Let Go and Let God. At around 10 pm, the phone rang. It was my realtor calling to tell me that the house was mine. Here is the kicker. I was not the highest bidder. There were two other bids that were significantly higher than mine. The owners wanted *me* to have the house. That was my evidence that my prayers worked.

I share this story to let you know that you don't have to use any particular form for your prayers. What you have to have is conviction about what you want. Prayer is not begging. It is not beseeching. At the same time, it is humble. Can you demand the good you want in your life from a place that is clear as a bell, humbly accepting, and not arrogant?

The trick to that is in the letting go. Many of us pray, do spiritual treatments, and practice the Law of Manifestation but don't get what we think we want. This could be because we actually do not let go of our need to control the results. I had absolutely no control over whether or not the sellers were going to choose me. I had to take all the steps, say my prayers, and let the results go. An important step in prayer is to let it go and let it be. The prayer, or what is called Spiritual Treatment used by Practitioners of Religious Science, for example, has a five-part process to it.

1. The recognition of the Higher Power, God, the Universe, by stating Its name.

2. The unification with that power by stating your connection to It.

3. The realization that your words carry the power to create your reality.

4. The thanks that you give to all that is good in your world.

5. The release that allows you to let go of the results and trust that God "Always says, Yes."

I use Spiritual Treatment daily with incredible results. More on this in a later chapter.

While I was writing this section on joy, an email popped up on my computer screen. It was from my friend, Paris Page, who is a Practitioner of Religious Science in the East Bay. His email included this quote:

If we wish to come to the Spirit for the healing of our wounds, let us come in peace and with spontaneous joy, for the Spirit is joy; let us come with thanksgiving also, for a thankful heart is in harmony with life.

– Ernest Holmes, *The Science of Mind*

EXERCISES

Mindfulness Practices

Practice mindfulness during the day in a form that appeals to you. Pick one of these, if it's hard to think of what to do:

Eat an apple with complete attention and focus on how it tastes, smells, the texture of it in your mouth, and the sounds it makes when you bite into it.

Brush your teeth noticing the smell of the toothpaste; how the brush bristles feel against your teeth and gums; the taste and consistency of the foam in your mouth; and the sounds that the bristles make as they scratch against your teeth.

Massage one of your hands with the other hand. Notice how each hand feels; the texture of your skin; the warmth or coolness of your hands; and what they look like.

Gratitude Practices

Keep a Gratitude Journal. You can use a beautifully bound journal or a simple lined notebook. Make a list each morning and each night of Ten Things I Am Grateful For.

Make a Gratitude Jar. You can use a beautiful jar or container or a simple, recycled pickle jar.

Put a label on it that says "Gratitude Jar."

Make the label colorful and delightful to look at.

Cut up strips of paper.

Every day, write out all the things you are grateful for on a strip of paper and put them in the jar.

At the end of the week, pull them all out and read them.

Start over.

Prayer Practices

Say, "Thank You!" throughout the day.

Create a prayer for yourself to say. Include the name of God that you use. Include a recognition that you are a part of God. State your intention clearly. Include what you are grateful for. Include your willingness to Let it Go and Let God. End with Amen! Ashe! or So Be It! Pray often.

(Optional: Find a piece of music that helps you feel your connection to God, the Universe, or your Higher Power – and listen to it often. Some that connect me are *Grace* by Snatam Kaur, *Sri Argala Stotram – Show Me Love* by Krishna Das, *Imagine Me* by Kirk Franklin, *The Spirit of God Is Upon Me* by Ricky Byers Beckwith, or the app on my phone, *Calm.)*

Before we move on, I want to take a moment to say, "Thank you" for reading my book! "Thank you!!"

Chapter Six

THE NEXT RIGHT THING

*You have to decide what your highest
priorities are and have the courage –
pleasantly, smilingly, non-apologetically,
to say "no" to other things.
And the way you do that is by having a
bigger "yes" burning inside.*
– Stephen R. Covey

So far we have examined some areas in your life where you might need to make decisions. There may be a whole host of others. Let's look at how to prioritize your tasks and ways to make decisions.

The everyday details of your life are likely to be dramatically different as a newly divorced person. You find yourself making decisions that during the marriage you consulted about, brainstormed about, or delegated to your partner and forgot about. Now they are all on you. This, in and of itself, can be a source of stress, anguish, or overwhelm. Simple tasks like grocery shopping can be fraught with challenging decisions if you are used to shopping for more than just yourself.

How many of the decisions that you made, like what kind of peanut butter to buy, were a compromised decision? Your partner wanted organic, but you have such fond memories of Skippy. Did you settle? Did you give up what you wanted? Did you compromise? What do you want now that you can make your own decision?

All these little decisions throughout the day are open for revision. That doesn't mean you have to make changes. It means that you have the opportunity to. There is massive freedom in that.

After years of being a vegetarian, I became a carnivore some years into my marriage. It was too much work to make two different meals. One of the first major decisions I made after my divorce was to return to being a vegetarian. Emotionally, it was easy. On a practical level, I had a lot of cans of tuna fish to get rid of. It felt like I was returning to myself in a small way.

Are there changes you made during your marriage that you want to reverse? Many things become habitual and can be harder to change. If you drank a glass of wine after work together, this may or may not be something you want to continue. Maybe now it feels too lonely or you worry about drinking alone. Do you even like drinking wine? Do you want to switch to red instead of white? What do *you* want?

It is a cleansing process to ask yourself what you want to be different in your new life, especially the things that are easily in your control. What type of toothpaste to get can be an easy decision if you disliked the one that you agreed to use as a couple. Other decisions may not be so clear. We will look at how to determine what is right for you below, but first, let's look at prioritizing your tasks.

Prioritizing

Before making major changes in your life, it is a good idea to prioritize your tasks. Steven Covey has a brilliant grid, called the Time Management Matrix, which he popularized in his book, *The Seven Habits of Highly Effective People*. I recommend using this matrix on the things in your life you want to change. There is an example of the Matrix in the Exercise section of this chapter. Here is a quick version of how it works.

The four categories on Covey's matrix are Urgent, Not Urgent, Important, and Not Important. They combine together so that you may have one task that is Urgent and Important, or another that is Urgent and Not Important. How you prioritize your tasks depends on which category it goes in. Urgent and Important tasks get to be first on your list, while Not Urgent and Not Important go last.

This may seem overly simple. It is. What can happen as we try to figure out what to do next, when there are so many things to do, is that they all *feel* like they are urgent and important. If you compare them to each other and stop for a minute to evaluate just how urgent or important they are, it will help you to sort through them. The urgent and important tasks are any that require immediate action. If you have to move out of your home in two weeks, then that is urgent and important. If, however, you would like to move because the home is too big for you and holds too many memories, that would likely be important but not urgent. Your exercise later in this chapter will ask you to make and prioritize your list of To-Dos using this matrix.

To Do Lists

I am a big fan of To Do lists and find them to be immensely helpful, not just for getting tasks accomplished but also for helping to create a sense of satisfaction and achievement. I have a couple of helpful hints about making and using To Do lists that I have been teaching for years to help my clients become more organized.

The first piece is to write all of your To Dos on one page. This could be in a daily calendar book, on a yellow, legal pad, or – if you are digitally inclined – in one place on your phone. Despite how much we love them, Post-it notes are not a good system for keeping track of what you need to do. They are fine to use for temporary reminders. Your day to day To Do list, however, needs to be in one place, not stuck all over your desk randomly.

Here is why. If you make an actual list and prioritize the list as described above, you have a script for your day, week, or month. It will help you keep on track when you get confused. It will be a guide when you are overwhelmed. It will show you what to do next.

At the same time, our To Do lists themselves can cause us to feel stressed. When they are three or four pages long, they can get pretty scary-looking. "How am I ever going to get any of that done?" we ask and then don't do anything. In Twelve Step programs, there is a slogan that is often used: "Do the next right thing."

For instance, when your mind is full of "what if's" and fears that this is all too much to cope with and you just want to crawl back into bed, pull the covers over your head, and wallow in your own misery, that is the time to tell yourself, "Okay, all I have to do now is the next right thing." The next right thing might be to take a shower. The next right thing after that might be to eat something. The next right thing after that might be to open the mail. One thing at a time. Steady as she goes. When I slow way down this way, it helps to manage my feelings of overwhelm, and at the same time, I get things done. None of these "next right things" may be on your actual To Do list. That is okay. Doing them moves you forward until you are able to pick one and start doing it. If you really want to slow things down, put them all on a To Do list. It might look like this:

Wake up
Take a shower
Feed the dog/cat/parakeet
Get dressed
Make coffee
Read the morning email/news/etc.
Walk the dog

Once you have completed a task on your To Do list, it is crucial that you check it off, cross it out, or in some way indicate that it's done. Why? Isn't that an extra step? Yes, it is. A hugely important step to show you tangibly all that you are doing. This simple practice will provide you with a sense of pride, accomplishment, and power. Check those things off as you do them. The act of checking them off is like taking a breath, patting yourself on the back and saying, "Good job." Give yourself that reward. You deserve it.

Once you have your To Do list and have it prioritized into what is Urgent and Important, etc., you want to look at it to see what you can delegate to someone else. We talk about delegation when we are at work, in terms of what we can give to our employees to do for us. This is not exactly what I mean by it. I mean what can you ask others to support you with in order to lighten your current burden? When you delegate to an employee they usually can't say, "No." If you attempt to delegate something to a family member, a friend or a neighbor, they totally have the right to say, "No."

A word about saying, "No" before we go on. I teach clients to post on their walls or to use as a mantra the words, "No is a complete sentence." Many of my clients, due to their well-meaning and helpful natures, have great difficulty saying, "No" without a lot of explanation and guilt. One woman told me she was afraid that if she said, "No" to her best friend without explaining why she didn't want to do what he had asked of her, that he would get mad at her and not like her anymore. She was afraid she would lose his friendship. I asked her if that friendship was worth her doing all the things she didn't want to do just to avoid saying, "No." She had to think about it for a while but decided to give it a try. It worked. The friend she said, "No" to without explanation responded with, "Okay. I just thought I'd ask." Remember this sentence during this time of needing others and also having way too much on your own plate. "No is a complete sentence." Whether you say it or someone says it to you. Practice saying it with no guilt and no extra energy. It is one of my favorite words. "Yes" is a great one, too.

If you are going to ask someone for help, you will want them to say, "Yes" to your request as often as possible. To make getting a "Yes" more likely, you want to use the same thinking that you would use at work when you decide who the best person is to delegate a task to. Ask yourself, who has the skill you need; the time to do the task; and for whom would it be most easy to do? Who would enjoy being helpful in your life? There are lots of people who love helping. Look for them. Identify them.

When you have figured out who can best support you in a task, write this person's name next to the item on your To Do list as a reminder to ask them. If they agree to take that task off your plate, definitely put their name next to it but don't check it off until you know it is done. I am not recommending nagging them about it. If they are someone who has a hard time saying, "No," it may show up as them not helping you. Don't trip. Ask someone else.

Once you've got your prioritized list, you will have some decisions to make. For example, one of the tasks on my list was whether to sell or keep my car. It wasn't fully paid for yet, so I had to be able to support the car payment. It also had been given to me by my ex, so I had to feel good driving it. I ultimately decided to keep it, as I loved it and was very clear that I did.

Some decisions might not be so clear-cut. You may feel ambivalent. Ambivalence is like being on a seesaw. You can make arguments for and against a decision that each have equal weight. I watched a client ask friends on Facebook which direction they should go with a big decision. All the well-meaning friends weighed in with varying answers. My client became more and more muddled by all these good pieces of advice. They increased her ambivalence. One of the crazy things about ambivalence is that sometimes when someone pushes us towards one side of the see saw, even if it is what we want to do, we go the other direction only because we felt pushed. It is so common to experience ambivalence when we want to change things that there is a whole therapeutic model designed to help people navigate it.

The techniques below will help you know what you want – what serves you. You will be able to stop spinning and make decisions with which you feel aligned.

Tools for Decision Making

On any regular day, there are so many decisions to make. It seemed to me that the transition from married to divorced added to them exponentially. Not having my partner as a sounding board was distressing. My self-doubt was at an all-time high, given I had clearly failed at marriage. How could I trust myself to make any good decisions? I found out initially that I actually couldn't. I made some doozies, mostly in the dating arena. Here are the tools I learned to use. They made it both easier to make decisions and more likely that the ones I made would actually support me in positive and healthy ways.

Flipping a Coin

You have done this. You get a coin, preferably a quarter. You decide that the head facing up means, "Yes" and the tail facing up means, "No." You ask a question that has a yes or no answer. You flip the coin. You get an answer. If it is heads up, the answer is yes. If it is tails up, the answer is no.

This is the decision making part. The goal of flipping the coin is to get the answer from deep inside you as to what *you* want, not from the randomness of the coin landing one way or the other. Here is what you do. As soon as the coin lands and you see that it said, "Yes" or "No," notice your emotional reaction. Did you feel a rush of relief? Did you feel a sinking feeling of disappointment? Did you yell, "Hell, no!" at the result or "Oh, God, yes!" Your emotional response is your answer. Not whatever the coin told you. Unless they agree with each other.

If you are disappointed that the coin told you "Yes," don't do it, whatever you asked about. If you are thrilled that it said, "Yes," get on it immediately. You want this.

Both this method and the muscle testing method below are ways to get an answer from your inner self that skips your logical mind. The logical mind, while very useful in logical and practical situations, can create some really interesting spinning when it tries to answer emotionally laden questions.

Muscle Testing

Muscle Testing, aka Applied Kinesiology, is a practice which helps you hear what your body wants/needs and what is good for you. It has been used by many health practitioners with positive results in treating such things as allergies. For our purpose, we are using it as a way to ask our body to tell us what it wants. Martha Graham, the world famous dancer and choreographer said, "The body never lies." Verbally, we lie to ourselves all the time. "That piece of cheesecake won't be bad for me," or "It won't hurt if I cheat on my diet today." If you ask yourself, using muscle testing, about that piece of cheesecake, it will likely tell you a different answer. In any case, it will tell you the truth. I find it to be more trustworthy than my best thinking. Again, a slogan from Twelve Step programs is apt. "My own best thinking got me here." If your best thinking gets you into states of confusion, messes you have to clean up later, or keeps you stuck, maybe it is time to rely on something else for answers.

Here's how muscle testing works. You first choose a method, of which there are a number. I am going to share about the method I use and like the best. You can view videos on YouTube about other methods if this one doesn't suit you. Muscle testing works with Yes or No questions.

It is best if you are rested, hydrated, and in a peaceful location. I have, however used this in my car (not while driving) or in the rest room at work to get quick answers.

Stand up, if you can. Sitting is also fine. You want your spine straight, your head up and your breathing easy.

Form a circle with your thumb and one of your fingers. I use my left hand, since I am right handed and my thumb and pointer finger to form the circle. Others like to use their ring or middle finger. Whatever feels comfortable to you is what is right for you.

Hold your hand with the formed circle up in front of you.

Take three deep breaths.

Take the pointer finger of your opposite hand and put it into the center of the circle with the side of the pointer finger resting against the juncture where the thumb and other finger join.

First you need to establish what a "Yes" and a "No" answer are. A "Yes" answer is when your thumb and finger hold the circle strongly. With a "No" answer, they cannot hold it. To establish the difference between the "Yes" and "No" you ask a question that you know is a Yes, such as, for me, "Is my name Marsha?" Using the side of the pointer finger of the opposite hand, you push against the juncture where the thumb and other finger meet. With a "Yes" answer, the fingers will stay joined.

Now ask yourself a question where you know the answer is "No." I would ask, "Is my name Joe?" Again use the side of the pointer finger to push against the juncture of thumb and finger. With a "No" answer, the fingers will part and the pointer finger will push through them. Since the body cannot lie, my fingers cannot retain their strong connection when I ask them if my name is Joe.

Try this with a few questions that you know are either Yes or No answers until you see how this works.

When you have established a Yes and No for yourself, you are ready to move on to a question that you aren't sure about. Close your eyes, take three breaths, form the circle and ask your question. Questions like:

"Should I take this job that I have been offered?"

"Is this the right place for me to live?"

"Should I call him (or her) back?"

Do not ask either/or questions like, "Should I take this job or that job?" Yes or No questions only. Notice the answer you get. Unlike the coin flip practice, muscle testing tends to be accurate with the answers. My common reaction to the answers I get when I use muscle testing is, "I knew that!" Because I did. My body knows what is right and good for me, even when I am logically trying to figure a way of doing something else. I taught both the Coin Toss and this practice to a fellow coach recently when she was struggling to decide whether or not to make a large financial investment in her business. In both instances, when she got the "Yes" answer, her response was, "I knew that!"

I learned the next practice from my friend Lucy. She uses it regularly when faced with a decision where she just can't make up her mind. There are two directions to go in, both seem to be equally good or equally bad. If you do muscle testing, a coin flip and keep getting a "Yes" but still can't seem to take the next step in that direction, this is a good practice to use.

Increase My Desire Prayer

This is a prayer, but you don't need to believe in God or a Higher Power to use it. You can be praying to your Self. It can be used for any place you feel stuck. Let's say you are struggling to figure out whether or not to move into a certain apartment. You have done all your background research on the neighborhood, the building, and the landlord. It is really attractive and within your budget. You flipped a coin, noticed that you wanted to move into it. You did muscle testing and got a strong "Yes" but you just can't pick up the pen and sign the lease papers. This is an agonizing place to be. Many of us have been there. We want something but can't seem to take the next step to make it so.

This is when to use this prayer. The prayer goes like this, "God (or whomever), please either increase my desire to move into this apartment now or decrease my desire to move into this apartment now. Give me a clear answer as to which way to go. Thank you!"

After you say the prayer, out loud, if possible, you let it go. Let Go and Let God, as the slogan says. Wait for an answer. It may not come immediately. The answer may come when you wake up the next day or when you are in the middle of cooking dinner. Suddenly, you will know what you need to do. You will feel a strong urge to either do it or not do it as your desire has either increased or decreased. Listen to it and take the action that your heart desires.

EXERCISE

To Do List

Make a list of all of the To Dos that need attention. Include those that must be done right away and those that are not as pressing. Get them all down on the list in whatever order they come out. You can add to the list in the days to come. It is a living document.

Look at each item on your list and rate them according to the Time Management Matrix below. Put a 1, 2, 3, or 4 next to each item.

Put them on your calendar in the order in which they need to be done. Be gentle with yourself. Do not give yourself more on any given day than you know you can handle, unless it is Urgent and Important. Sometimes we have to bite the bullet and push through for these items but when you can, please allow yourself the space to do what needs to be done in a way that is kind to yourself.

If you have a couple of items on your prioritized list and are not sure which to do first, you can use Muscle Testing to answer the question, "Should I do X before Y?" For any of the items that you are stuck about, you can use the Increase My Willingness Prayer to help get you unstuck.

If you make these practices a part of your daily life going forward, they will continue to serve you. They did for me.

Time Management Matrix

	URGENT	NOT URGENT
IMPORTANT	Crises Deadlines **Do First - #1**	Long term goals Recreation Relationship building Prevention activities Personal growth Recognizing new opportunities **Do Next - #2**
NOT IMPORTANT	Emails Some meetings Some activities **Do Late or Delegate - #3**	Time wasters Facebook, etc. Busy work **Don't Do or Ignore - #4**

(Optional: Music to listen to while creating your list: *Getting It Done* by Ron Gelinas.)

Chapter Seven

WHO ARE YOU ANYWAY?

*Open your eyes and see that you are far more
than you imagine.
You are the world, you are the universe; you
are yourself and everyone else, too!
It's all the marvelous Play of God.
Wake up, regain your humor.
Don't worry, just be happy. You are already free!*

*– Dan Millman, Way of the Peaceful Warrior: A Book
That Changes Lives*

After you complete the exercise in the last chapter, you will have a nice list of things to do. Congratulations! My next question for you is: Who is going to be doing those tasks? Who are you, anyway? This chapter is set up to be a series of short writing exercises that will help you answer that question.

You are not the same person who took those vows and lived in a marriage for however long you did. You are not the same person who took the steps to divorce. You are a newly forming you. Every morning we wake up, we are a new version of ourselves, even if only slightly. Today, you are a new you who you haven't been before. It is a great practice to keep asking yourself, "Who am I anyway?" See what answers arise.

My mother told me I was bossy as a young girl. I am the oldest of four. I did love to tell my siblings what games we were going to play and how we were going to play them. Kind of bossy, huh? I judged that part of myself, especially during my marriage, where it had very little outlet, as it was usually his way or the highway. Bossy was a bad, bad thing. I was also called "shy" by lots of people for most of my younger life and encouraged to speak up, stop hiding, and to not be so shy.

What if instead of being bossy, I was a natural born leader who had wonderful ideas to share? What if I viewed it that way? That feels dramatically different. What if instead of being shy, I was deeply sensitive and needed time to adjust to new things and people? I could feel empathy for myself instead of disdain.

What identities have others given you now or in the past? What words have they used to describe you? Very importantly, who do you tell yourself that you are? Among other things, I am a private, sensitive, thoughtful, and considerate person who is spiritually focused, a vegetarian, an animal right's activist, and an author who hates driving. Who are you?

Pick up your journal and make a quick list of adjectives that you and others have used to describe you. Write down the ones you like and the ones you don't. Don't think too much. Just jot them down. If we were in person, I'd just ask you to rattle them off to me. This is how we make ourselves up every day. We create our identities with all these labels and likes and dislikes. Some of them change over time; some change often; some remain with us for life. What are yours?

Take the list you wrote. Ask yourself the following question, "Which of these is 100 percent true about who I know myself to be?" Don't hide. Circle them, even if you don't like them. Let's forget for now about the ones you don't believe represent you. For example, my ex called me all kinds of names and saw horrid things in me that I know for sure don't live in me. They were instead parts of him. His rage was *his* rage, but he liked calling me "angry" when I wasn't. Don't spend time trying to figure out if these are true or not.

Let's take the circled items on your list and (as we call it in the therapy world) reframe them. To reframe something is to consciously change the way it is considered or expressed. It is what I did when I changed the way I considered being bossy. I reframed it to being a leader.

Write next to each item a reframe of the characteristics that are less than flattering. For instance, bossy = leader; shy = sensitive; noisy = exuberant; secretive = private; emotional = in touch with your feelings.

Notice how it feels to look at your list after you have reframed the items on it. Put them together in a sentence and say them to yourself. Can you stand with your head up and say proudly, out loud, "I am a private, sensitive woman who is in touch with her feelings," if those are on your list? Try it. You can also write it out and post it on your bathroom mirror as a daily reminder. It is useful to keep reminding ourselves of the qualities that we reframe so that the next time a person calls you "secretive" you can say, "Thanks, but actually I'm a very private person."

A fun but sometimes misleading way to get feedback on who you are is by taking online assessments. One that I have found to be accurate was created by Sally Hogshead. It is a test called the *Fascination Personality Test,* which measures how other people in the world see you and what fascinates them about you. Her assessment of me put me in the category of being the Change Agent, which is exactly why I am writing this book: to help you change the things in your life that are not serving you anymore. Because it is not always easy to see yourself objectively, there are benefits to asking someone who knows you well what word they would use to describe you. A woman who I coached recently allowed me to provide her with a list of her attributes and skills, which were immensely helpful in updating her resume. She had not considered for herself some of the attributes that I could clearly see in her.

Let's look more deeply into the qualities of yourself you may not like much.

Character Defects, Character Assets, and Superpowers

I draw again on Twelve Step recovery programs for guidance. People who are in recovery from addictions of any sort have a humongous task of re-inventing themselves and restoring their identities. In Steps Four, Five, and Six of the Twelve Steps, the process of recovery requires the person to take an inventory of all of their character defects, share them with someone else, and then give them to God for healing and release. This is a profound renewal process and causes us to take a deep look at who we are; who we have been; who we have hurt; and who we want to be going forward.

A valuable teaching from these steps is the idea that on the flip side of every so-called "defect" there lives a vital asset. For example, let me share about one of mine: perfectionism, which has been a burr in my side for most of my life. Perfectionism has caused me to worry unnecessarily; to be harsh with myself when I make a mistake; and to judge others fiercely when they make mistakes. I am the person who adjusts the picture frames in a room when they are slightly off kilter. In general, this characteristic has blocked the closeness that I can experience toward others as no relationship or shared experience is ever perfect. My judgmental mind is always looking for what is wrong with each situation and is expert at finding things to label as "wrong."

The flip side of perfectionism is valuing excellence. If I take the judgment out of it, perfectionism can convert easily to a motivator for me to push on and do an excellent job. Because I can see all the things that are not perfect easily, this skill gives me an ability to find opportunities to improve things that others might miss. When I set up my system for online coaching calls, I noticed that the computer screen reflected in my eyeglasses so brightly that the other person on the call could not see my eyes. This is not good for doing one-on-one coaching. You should be able to see my eyes and not bright, shining, alien-looking squares. I noticed it on the first call I made. My client did, too. I asked the software sales person what could be done about this. He had never noticed it. In fact, one of the videos he used to demonstrate the product showed a co-worker's glasses reflecting the screen so brightly that you could not see his eyes. This may not be a fix for the software designer to take on. They could advise people in their sales calls about it to help them avoid this issue up front. It was an opportunity for improvement, which I was able to point out to him.

Can you look at the items on your list and find ways in which they serve you if you flip them to an asset? My colleague, Tish, often says that the experiences she had in her life that were traumatizing gave her superpowers. Her ultra-sensitivity and ability to immediately grasp other people's emotional states before they even know what they are feeling kept her safe and alive as a child. Today it is one of her superpowers as a therapist. She can read people's emotional energy like a wizard.

What are your superpowers? Which of the challenging parts of your personality have real ways in which they serve you and others for good? To answer this question, you will need to listen deeply to yourself and not so much to the voices of others, whether you hear them in your head or in real life. I like this quote, which describes the state we want to be in when we look at ourselves deeply:

Create loving energy around yourself. Love your body, love your mind. Love your whole mechanism, your whole organism. By "love" is meant, accept it as it is. Don't try to repress. We repress only when we hate something, we repress only when we are against something. Don't repress, because if you repress, how are you going to watch? And we cannot look eye to eye at the enemy; we can look only in the eyes of our beloved. If you are not a lover of yourself you will not be able to look into your own eyes, into your own face, into your own reality.

– Osho, Love, Freedom, and Aloneness; The Koan of Relationships

Look into your face, into your reality and see who you are right now. The good, great, not so good, awful, creepy, tired, and wonderful you. Can you accept who you see? Can you name and own all of your "defects," assets, and super-powers? Are you willing to love yourself with all of them? Return to the Prayer for the Increase in Willingness if you want help with this.

There is another way to examine who you are which involves your likes and dislikes

Attraction and Repulsion (or Likes and Dislikes)

In Chapter Six, The Next Right Thing, you learned how to use muscle testing to determine the things that are healthy for you and how to make a decision about them. If you pay daily attention to what you like and don't like – or even more strongly, what you are attracted to and repulsed by – this notic-ing will provide you with information about who you are now. Not necessarily in the ways you might think.

Not all the things that you are attracted to may be good or helpful for you. If you use the muscle testing practice, it can sort for you. I absolutely love pizza. I become almost weak in the knees when I smell it. The attraction feels magnetic. At the same time, it is so disruptive to my digestion that if I eat even a slice my stomach will blow up with gas and make me look like I am seven months pregnant. I also have a history of being romantically attracted to alcoholics and addicts. In case you wondered where all the Twelve Step references are coming from, I came by them honestly, by working the steps myself. What I learned is that I am much better at using my love for alcoholics and addicts to help them professionally than I am at, for instance, being married to one. I can honor my attraction and make sensible decisions about it.

Because you are wide open to the possibility of becoming a new you as a result of this massive change in your status, this is the time to pay attention to what you are attracted to and to what repulses you. Get curious about it. How have the things you are attracted to in the past served you? How have the things you have been repulsed by stopped you?

A client, Sheila, shared with me about a co-worker, Joan. Joan was driving her crazy. She couldn't even bear being in the same room with her. Sheila was utterly repulsed by everything about Joan; her voice; what she spoke about; the ways she expressed herself; even how she ate her lunch. I suggested gently to Sheila that she might have a lot in common with Joan and that her dislike could be coming from not liking those things about herself. In therapist speak, we talk about projecting the unwanted parts of ourselves onto others in order to reject them. For example, if you are disgusted by people who overeat in public, I would guess that you have a harsh judgment about yourself whenever you overeat, if you even let yourself. You may have a loud inner critic shouting out that, "That is disgusting!" Not a friendly, compassionate voice to listen to, is it?

At first, Sheila did not want to accept that she was in any way, shape, or form like Joan. She rejected the idea outright. I gave her the assignment to say something friendly to Joan every day. To find something that she honestly could say she liked about her and to say it to her. It could be as simple as, "I like your earrings." It did need to be authentic. She agreed begrudgingly and made it a daily practice. It was only a matter of a week before she confided in me that she thought she actually did like Joan; that she wasn't so bad after all. Today, they are close friends. This kind of magic can happen when we become curious about our attractions, repulsions, and what they do for us.

Our likes and dislikes also guide who we let into our lives as we now create a new version of our social world.

Finding Your New Tribe

Much has been written about finding your tribe. I hope you have already found yours. If you have, keep adding to it. Grow it. As you get older, the bigger it is, the longer it lasts. When we divorce, we often lose members of our tribe or even are cast out from what we thought was our tribe. I lost all contact with my ex-husband's family after my divorce, which was a further heartbreaking loss. I was not ready to join the tribe of over-40 divorced women as a replacement for being a part of that family. No way did I want that to be my identity. It brought all the shame of the failure of my marriage right up to the surface. It was like wearing a badge that said, "Failed at marriage."

Who better though to understand this dark and enlightening passage than women who are in it themselves? There are support groups for the newly divorced for a reason. It is a hard passage to make on your own. Brutal, painful, lonely, and totally unnecessary to do by yourself. This is a time in life when you need support, holding, coaching, and comfort. You need to feel like you belong somewhere and with others. Family bonds can become tighter as you lean on them for this. They can also become strained if they didn't approve of the divorce. Connection is key. You have just suffered a huge disconnection. How to get reconnected and who to connect with is one of the pressing questions. Professional therapists, especially those with experience in grief, loss, and divorce can help a lot. You may feel the need for more than a once-a-week group or a once-a-week therapy session. I know I did.

Who are your people right now? Who is there to support you, day and night? Who totally gets what you are going through? Who will help you, no questions asked? Who do you have the courage to show your needy, broken self to? Please make a list of these wonderful people with their phone numbers and email addresses to keep with you at all times. Let them know how much you appreciate them. Leave any feelings of guilt or "I don't deserve this," out of it. People love to help each other when we're in pain. In fact, one of the recommended things to do to alleviate depression is to find someone else to help. This may not be the time for you to take on any additional caregiving, as you are in need your-self. Instead, know that in asking for help from your tribe members that you are actually giving them a gift. The gift of being useful. The gift of helping.

I took a break from writing this chapter to get a short chair massage at my local health food store. My neck, shoulder, hands, and arms were tense from hours of typing. The man who worked the knots out with great care volunteered to give me extra free "bonus" minutes. I, of course, accepted and laughingly replied, "Oh, you can tell how much stress is in me right now, huh?" He said quietly, "No, I just like being useful."

Let your friends, family members, and other folks in your tribe be useful to you. At the same time, keep exploring and looking around for new people to bring into your tribe. As you are forming a new you, the people you are attracted to and with whom you want to spend time is likely to change. Let it do so. Follow your inner guidance if it tells you to check out the new art gallery or music venue. Go and see who you meet. There are meet-up groups for almost everything. Experiment. See where you feel at home or at the very least, less alone.

One of the things I did in my first year after divorce was join Meetup.com. I signed up for hikes, bike rides, and various events with groups of strangers. They were fun but didn't help me expand my circle in any meaningful way. That is, until I signed up to go to a zydeco dance. I had never even heard of it before but it sounded interesting. I had always loved to dance but didn't do it much during my marriage. Zydeco is a type of syncopated music and the dance style that goes with it. It is happy, upbeat, and very fast. The dance form, except for the line dances, is a partner dance with a lead and a follow. It swept me up and swept me into a rich, cultured community of musicians, dancers, and artists. As BB King sang, "I found my thrill …" in the zydeco community.

Not all of us have an easy time finding our tribes and especially during a trying time like after a divorce. If you have tried to fit into several groups over time and none of them really clicked and felt like home, you may feel a little gun-shy about participating in any group situations at all. Something will come of even these attempts. For me, it was finally realizing that I needed to form and lead my own tribe. I wasn't meant to join someone else's for longer than it took me to gain the knowledge and connection that group could provide. This was an empowering realization as it shifted me from seeking to belong to deciding to create.

Do you have a creative leader in you who has been chomping at the bit to come out and run freely? This is a process I can help you explore. You can email me at marsha@ marshavaughn.com.

In the next chapter we will look at further practices you can use in this path to loving your new self. Before that, here is your current exercise.

EXERCISE

This chapter has had multiple exercises throughout. Review your lists. Your qualities, likes, and dislikes, your superpowers, and your tribe members.

Find a photo of yourself that you like. It is best if this is a recent photo.

Make a collage by pasting the photo of yourself in the center of a board.

Surround yourself with photos of the people in your tribe. If you don't have current photos of them, you might be able to find some to print from their Facebook pages or other social media.

Either cut your list of words describing your reframed attributes and superpowers out of magazines or type them up in Word, using cool fonts. Print these and glue them on all around your photo.

We are going to make another collage to manifest what you want in your life later. This is not that. This is a visual representation of who your best self is today and who your helpers are.

Hang the collage some place where you can see it often.

Greet yourself warmly each time you look at it. "Looking good there!"

(Optional: Listen to songs that affirm your self-love. Chaka Khan, *I Love Myself* and Mary J. Blige, *Love Yourself* are good places to start.)

Chapter Eight

PRACTICE MAKES IMPERFECT

*An ounce of practice is generally worth more
than a ton of theory.*

*– Ernst F. Schumacher, Small Is Beautiful: A Study of
Economics as if People Mattered*

I hope you have started some of the practices in the exercises.
Moving forward as the new you with grace and ease does
require practice. Old habits die hard. We can make an external
change but then not feel any different on the inside. That is
where practice comes in.

The concept of "practice making perfect" is kind of lame,
in my humble opinion. I don't like the idea of perfection in
the first place so why would I want to practice to get *there?*
As I said, one of my character defects has been perfectionism. Totally crazy-making. At the same time, I was annoyed
when I realized that I had to do all this stuff just to keep my
head above water. I was not an easy convert to the concept
of practicing.

For six months after my divorce, I woke up an hour early
every morning. I journaled for 30 minutes first thing when

I woke up. After that, I read a chapter of Pema Chodron's book, *When Things Fall Apart*. They are short chapters and I'm a fast reader so that didn't take long. I sat in meditation after that for 20 minutes. During the day, I said my gratitude list often and said, "Thank You" all the time. Before bed, I expressed more gratitude followed by forgivenesses and prayers. My whole day was full of practices, and I wasn't even at a monastery or studying yoga.

At times, I felt such resentment because it seemed to me that those ubiquitous "other people" didn't have to do anything just to stay in neutral. Some people seemed like they just woke up joyful and stayed that way all day. I hated them. It was just way too easy for them. In my judgment of them lay another way I was separating myself from others and disconnecting. This added to, instead of alleviated, my grief and loss.

What I began to notice is all the practicing I was doing, even resentfully at first, started to make a difference in how I was viewing my life. Slowly, slowly, I began to actually enjoy doing them instead of gritting my teeth and struggling to think of one thing I was grateful for. I noticed the feelings of lightness that arose every so often. Trust me, it was not all sweetness and light. Sometimes what came to the forefront was anger and grief in loud and noticeable ways.

Two of the practices that were the most challenging for me, but may be a breeze for you, were meditation and forgiveness. One at a time, let's look at what they have to offer. We will end this chapter with some easy and fun practices.

Meditation

We can spend our whole lives escaping from
the monsters of our minds."

— Pema Chodron, When Things Fall Apart: Heartfelt
Advice for Hard Times

I highly recommend Pema's book for instructions on how to meditate. It is not my task here to teach you how to do it. Instead, I want to encourage you to find the barriers in you to adopting it as a practice and help you to drop them so that you can integrate it into your life as one of your regular practices.

Our minds can lead us around on a very short leash and make us extremely miserable. All of our fears and projections, worries and needs, judgments and distractions cycle through our minds all day long, non-stop. This has been described by Buddhists as "monkey mind." It is also a bit like watching laundry go around in the washing machine. There's a sock. Now, a sheet turned inside out. There's my black t-shirt.

When I first sat in meditation, I believed that the goal was to have no thoughts at all and have a blank mind. So of course, when my mind started doing the washing machine thing and distracting me with all kinds of stories, ideas, memories, or plans, I thought I wasn't meditating right. I wasn't doing it perfectly or else I would have had a still mind. As a result of this relentless quality of my mind to distract me, I actually tried about 10 different times over the course of about 15 years to become someone who regularly meditated. Each time after a short while, I gave up, thinking it was pointless. I was never going to tame that chatter.

When I read Pema's book, I finally grasped that the practice was to notice those crazy, relentless thoughts and accept them. I did not need to stop them. I am certain that all of the other meditation teachers I listened to previously had said the same thing. It wasn't until I read it in her book that I got it. She gave me permission to do it imperfectly. She taught me how to practice.

Meditation practice is not about later,
when you get it all together and you're
this person you really respect.
– Pema Chodron, *The Pocket Pema Chodron*

As a practice, meditation is probably the most all-encompassing. It takes a daily regular commitment to it. It also takes a teacher. The timing of who that teacher is will be right on time for you. I encourage you to look for one. Who can give you permission to learn to meditate, to begin at the beginning, make mistakes, and still accept and love yourself? Each of us will read or hear meditation teachers differently. Look around and find yours. Now let's talk about forgiveness.

Forgiveness

You have no doubt heard forgiveness recommended as a good thing to do to heal from the past; to let go of your abuser; to clean the slate; or to reclaim your life. Forgiveness and blame are flip sides of the same coin. If I blame someone for hurting me or for leaving me, and I know that I am right because they actually did do that, why on God's earth would I ever want to forgive them? Pretty good question. I might prefer to find a way to hurt them back instead or at least hold them in my mind with hatred and disdain as if that was hurting them. If you are doing this toward anyone, but especially towards your ex-partner since we are working with divorce here, ask yourself this question. How is it hurting that person for you to be hating them? Really? In their everyday life, while they are eating breakfast or driving to work, how is your hatred of them impacting them? When they are getting ready for bed, sending some emails, or even out on a date with someone else, how are your hateful thoughts making any difference to them? Guess what? They aren't. Your hatred is not poisoning their well. It is not causing them to have a restless night's sleep. They are not losing weight and feeling sick over it. They are not spending their waking moments thinking about how much you hate them and how they did you wrong.

Who is being impacted? You. Watch yourself every time you remember some particularly nasty memory. Watch the anger or pain surge through your body and the litany of blame that follows from that. Your stomach gets upset, not theirs. You have a hard time focusing on work. They don't. You toss and turn at night. They sleep like a baby.

It's not fair. I know. This might make you hate them even more. How could they do what they did and get off scot-free? They deserve punishment, you think. Maybe they do. Maybe they don't. Let's not go there. The point of forgiveness is to let go of all the ways in which we hurt ourselves by holding on to these stories, judgments, and hatreds. If it is never going to actually punish them or even out the scale of hurt, then why keep it going?

You forgive others for you. It is a purely selfish thing to do. It is not about them. Forgiveness allows you to drop the rope and move on. It opens the door for you to see the lesson and let go of the pain. It is one of the hardest things that I have ever done. I couldn't do it alone. I needed others to be there and talk it through because my anger kept bringing me back to self-righteous resentment and the need for revenge.

A few words about saying, "I'm sorry," while we are on the topic of forgiveness. Other than to apologize for hitting someone accidentally with your chair or spilling water on their table in a restaurant, the words, "I'm sorry," are not very useful. They do help us feel better from an accidental occurrence like I just described. But, when a partner is unfaithful in a marriage; verbally abuses you; physically hurts you; steals from you; destroys your property; or commits any of the other grievous acts that sometimes happen in marriage, no amount of saying, "I'm sorry" will rectify it.

What can make a difference is making amends. I want to know what my partner is going to do differently the next time. I want to see amends not hear apologies. Making amendments to your behavior means making changes to it. If someone is truly committed to fixing a relationship or situation, they will change their behavior and it won't matter whether or not they say the words, "I'm sorry."

To begin the practice of forgiveness, I recommend having a person you feel safe with to start the conversation. This is an ongoing, deep process that does not happen overnight. Forgiveness takes time. It can be painful. For this reason, many of us avoid it. Who wants to jump head first, knowingly, into something that is going to hurt? But, what if it brought immense amounts of relief and joy as a result? Would it be worth it then? Start with the easier things, the low-hanging fruit. It was easier for me to forgive my ex-husband for the things he did as a result of not being willing to own his own gayness because I could see that those actions weren't about me in any way. It was harder, much harder, to forgive him for the ways he hurt me verbally and physically. Those seemed personal. It took some work to see that they were coming from the same place in him and also were not about me. I made the decision not to have further contact with him, as he did not amend his behavior. He never did become a safe person for me. At the same time, despite never having contact with him again, I was able to reach a place of forgiveness where I no longer wished him ill but instead prayed for his wellbeing and peace.

There are some things to remember about forgiveness. It doesn't mean for a minute that what they did was okay. You are not forgetting it and saying, in effect, "no big deal." It also doesn't mean that you have to let the other person into your life again or have any contact with them. It is not about them. It is about you and healing your heart. As with most kinds of healing, it happens in increments with daily doses of the appropriate medicine – in this case, forgiveness. When we are able to forgive someone, we stop seeing them as monsters and stop giving them that degree of control over us. We can see them as fallible humans. We can fly freely.

Equally as important as forgiving others – is forgiving ourselves. When a marriage dissolves, it can feel like we are a failure and all of those self-judgments can come hailing down on our head. I heard the, "What is wrong with you? How could you be so stupid?" voice for quite some time as my marriage crumbled. I had a lot of self-forgiveness I needed to offer myself in order to be able to accept truly that I did the best I could with what I had at the times I made the decisions that I made. Getting the lesson means that next time I will be more aware and make different decisions. Can you forgive yourself for the decisions you made, the things you did or didn't do in your marriage? Can you do it without blaming your partner? It is not forgiving yourself to say, "I forgive myself for the marriage ending because he was the one who broke it in the first place." That ain't it. Forgiving yourself sounds more like, "I forgive myself for all the times I allowed myself to not stand up for what I really wanted and believed." Or "I forgive myself for all of the times that I didn't take care of myself and keep myself safe."

I have used this practice with clinicians I have supervised. A supervisee, Charles, had a thought that he didn't do enough in his work with his clients. He is and was one of the hardest working therapists. He goes all out for his clients. He felt so weighted by this thought that he felt like he could never do enough for them. It got to the point where one of his clients yelled at him, "You don't help me enough," each time they met. I helped him to examine this and see that his thoughts and his guilt about it were producing this internal stress and this external result. As he shifted his thinking and forgave himself, his client began to yell at him less. Forgiveness can be magical like that.

> (Optional exercise: A song I love to listen to that gets me in the space of forgiveness and openness is *May the Long Time Sun Shine Upon You* by Snatam Kaur.)

There is an expression I like, "What you focus on, expands." What this means is this. If you focus your energy and thoughts on resentment, hatred, and all of the broken areas in your life, what will happen is that similar feelings and experiences will expand and show up in your life. You will get more resentment, hatred, and ugly stuff.

An embarrassing example in my life proved this to me when I was walking down Third Avenue in New York City. I had been stood up by a client and was furious about it. A lot was going on in my life and this was the last straw. I am not a person who explodes when angry but more often goes into a quiet simmering place. I have never been someone who gets into physical fights with others. As I stormily stomped back through the rush-hour crowds on the street to the subway, a woman brushed against me going in the opposite direction. She bumped into me hard. She turned and glared at me, her anger being as big as mine. I didn't say anything and kept walking. My look back at her was so filled with the anger I was feeling about my client not showing up that she took it as a threat. She jumped me from behind as I walked away. What happened next was crazy. She pummeled me in full view of hundreds of passerby, none of whom stepped in to help me. I, not being a fighter, could do nothing but cry for help. After she wrestled me around a few times, a man finally stepped in and ordered her to leave me alone. She stormed off. I went home shakily trying to figure what that was all about.

It was about *my* anger. Focusing on my anger, as I had, caused it to expand in such a way that I literally got into a fight with another woman. This has never happened again, thankfully, as when I feel myself fill with anger like that I have found outlets that dissipate it quickly and effectively.

If you fill your days with gratitude and forgiveness as opposed to anger and revenge thoughts, you will find more of that showing up in your daily life. More of the good stuff. That is a lot more enjoyable to invite in. This can look like being appreciated by people at work or the driver at the crossroads allowing you to go first. I suggest inviting graciousness into your life as often as you can by tuning your frequency to gratitude and forgiveness.

Self-Care Practices

Here are practices I recommend you make a regular part of your life going forward. Self-care practices are things you can use all the time to make you feel good, connected, relaxed, and in touch with yourself. Both meditation and forgiveness are self-care practices that I hope you will adopt daily. They require more from us than the ones I'm about to describe.

Bathing

If you live in Maui, I would recommend daily swimming. If you don't live where you can spend time in the sea, the next best thing is to take baths. Hot, cold, lukewarm, doesn't really matter. With or without bubbles or smelling salts doesn't either. The body responds to being immersed in water in a profoundly relaxing and restorative way. If you don't have a bathtub, showers work, too. Differently, but the water will cleanse you – both your body and your energy. The bathtub or shower is the absolute best place to cry.

Crying

Yes, I am going to recommend crying as a practice. I often tell clients to never miss an opportunity to cry. I have seen them burst into tears due to a tragic loss and apologize for crying. Really??! You are apologizing to me for crying when you just found out that someone you love has cancer?!

You never need to apologize for crying. Yes, it makes other people uncomfortable. It activates the mirror neurons in their brains and makes them want to cry, too. That is a good thing. That is how we empathize with, care for, and connect with one another. At a staff meeting I facilitated, half of the team cried due to a beloved staff member leaving. No, they were not falling apart and sobbing. But they let the tears flow unashamedly as they expressed their appreciation for the person who was leaving their team. How lovely and how loving. It is one of my aspirations to create places where it is safe to cry wherever I go. If it is safe to cry, it is safe to be vulnerable which means it is safe, period.

Flowers and Incense

Did you know that your sense of smell is connected to the part of the brain that processes emotions and memory? If you read, or tried to read, Marcel Proust's *Remembrances of Things Past*, you will have seen how a simple cookie can bring someone back through time. We have emotional associations to scented flowers, perfumes, laundry soaps, foods, doggy smell, new car odor, and many other things. What scents do you absolutely love? The ones that make you go, "Ahhhh," with pleasure? For me, it is any type of jasmine flower, roses, and sandalwood incense. I keep a stick of incense by my computer. Not burning. Available for quick sniffs as I'm typing. Find the things you love to smell and fill your environment with them. You can buy essential oils in many scents. A friend discovered by accident that mixing peppermint oil with orange oil was both relaxing and stimulating. Now she carries a little bottle with her everywhere.

Walking

Walking as a practice is a combination of physical exercise and meditation. I wear a Fitbit to track my steps. That is the exercise part. It encourages me to keep taking steps to meet the goal I set. It helps me pay attention to how many steps I take per day and how many staircases I go up and down. When we pay attention to something, we can make decisions about it. Like upping our goals. The meditation part of walking involves paying attention to where you are and what is around you. It is astonishing the number of people I see daily who walk and text or read Facebook on their phones. They literally have no idea what is around them or, in some cases, where they are. Despite the warnings about this not being safe, people continue to do it. If this is you, you will need to put your phone away to practice the type of walking I am about to describe.

Thich Nhat Hahn wrote an entire book called *Walking Meditation*, which is a How To book on this. I highly recommend it. Or you can start now, by putting the phone away and just walking. Walk slowly with attention to where you are and what is around you. Walking like this is not about getting somewhere other than where you are. It is about noticing where you are. You know how people say, "Stop and smell the roses?" Do it. If you are passing a neighbor's garden or a flower stand, stop. Take it in and enjoy it. Pay attention to your connection to the earth while you walk. It is hard to feel through our shoes and on concrete. Much easier when we are barefoot on the sand at the ocean. We want to recreate that lovely feeling of walking barefoot with the sand squishing through our toes. Find a place to take daily walks where you can feel this delightful connection. Walk there for at least a half an hour.

EXERCISE

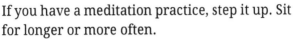

If you have a meditation practice, step it up. Sit for longer or more often.

If you don't have one, find a meditation teacher. You can find a book, a YouTube video, or an actual teacher. Learn the practice that feels right for you. Practice it daily.

Make a list of the people in your life that you would like to forgive. Put yourself at the top of the list. Find a safe person to practice forgiveness with, who understands how it works. This is an area I can help you through. If you want to work with me on it, contact me at marsha@marshavaughn.com.

Integrate as many of the self-care practices into your life as you can. Please don't make excuses like, "I don't have time." If you don't have time to care for yourself, what exactly are you doing with yourself? You can't help others or make progress in your life if you don't operate with a full tank. Fill those tanks with self-care and self-love. You can do this!

Chapter Nine

THE CHOICE

Half of all marriages end in divorce – and then there are the really unhappy ones.

– Joan Rivers

Being divorced is like being hit by a Mack truck. If you live through it, you start looking very carefully to the right and to the left.

– Jean Kerr

If you made a list of the reasons why any couple got married,
and another list of the reasons for their divorce,
you'd have a ... lot of overlapping.

– Mignon McLaughlin

This chapter starts with jokes about divorce and marriage because humor is a healing tool. Next, I am going to ask you some deep questions that aren't humorous. I started with humor to remind you to find something to laugh about if your pondering gets too heavy. I use my little dog's antics as a regular comic break.

We will examine your thoughts about marriage, divorce, failure, and being single. We are looking at your thoughts because you can change those in a heartbeat. My aim is to deepen your insight into yourself and your choices.

Marriage

Let's start with marriage. We've all heard the horrible statistics about marriage. The Center for Disease Control and Prevention reports that while 6.9 out of 1,000 people get married, 3.2 out of 1,000 of us get divorced. If this is so, why in the world do we keep getting married? Why do we believe in it – as something that everyone should do at least once – and hope that we beat the odds? You will find religious, political, and family answers to this question. What I am curious about is what *your* beliefs are? What were your thoughts about marriage? Why did you get married? This is a good journaling exercise. What comes right off the top of your head?

Easy answers are, "We were in love," "I wanted to have a family," "Everyone in my family is married. My parents expected me to," or "He/She asked...." These don't go very deep and clearly are not sustainable enough reasons to overturn the statistics cited above.

 EXERCISE

Take ten minutes with your journal and ask yourself these questions. Write down whatever comes up:

✓ Why did I get married?

✓ What did I think would be different once I was married?

✓ What does marriage mean to me?

✓ What did I think that marriage would provide for me?

✓ What would I have as a married person that I did not have as a single person?

✓ Why did I *really* get married?

I want you to get your own answer to this to help you see that marriage was a choice you made in order to meet these goals or fulfill these beliefs. Your thoughts about marriage produced a result. Now let's ask the same questions about divorce.

✓ Why did I get divorced?

✓ What did I think would be different once I was divorced?

✓ What does divorce mean to me?

✓ What did I think that divorce would provide for me?

✓ What would I have as a divorced person that I did not have as a married person?

✓ Why did I *really* get divorced?

Looking back at the Mignon McLaughlin quote above, can you see any overlaps? For me, one of the reasons I got married was that I didn't want to be alone anymore. One of the reasons

I got divorced was because I discovered that I was actually lonelier in the marriage than I had been when I was single. I saw that being alone was much better than being lonely and not at all the same thing. My thought that marriage would cure loneliness was an error in my thinking.

The big existential question you might ask yourself is, "Why get married anyway?" If you have beliefs that are deep in your core about the necessity of marriage, my aim is not to overturn them but to help you get curious about them. Are there any of the things on your Why I Got Married list that you could have or even do have as a divorced or previously single person? Did marriage change anything? If so, what?

The biology behind love and having children is fascinating to study. What if your whole drive towards love, marriage, and having children was driven by hormones designed to assure the survival of our species? Not a very romantic idea, is it? When we are in the throes of romantic attraction to someone, it can feel cosmic, "meant to be," and as if it is the sole purpose of our life. What if we are being manipulated or tricked by our own brain and hormones into making decisions that are not the best for us as a fully actualized human but are great to keep the human race going? Research has been conducted on both humans and animals to determine how pheromones cause us to make decisions. From gay men choosing other gay men based on the scent of their sweat to heterosexual men feeling less physical attraction after smelling women's tears, some unique ideas have been demonstrated. In order to understand who we are attracted to, researchers found that women tend to prefer the body odor of men whose chemical makeup is different from their own because they would produce healthier babies with these men. What if we choose our partners based on this instead of on who will provide us with the most fulfilling relational attachment?

Can you think of people who made decisions to get married based on what appeared to you from the outside to be irrational reasons such as love or wanting to have his babies? From the outside you could see that it was not going to work out as they dreamed? This is what I mean. Our chemistry can drive us to make decisions that lead to heartbreak.

Divorce

What about your thoughts on divorce? It is my hope that in doing these exercises, you will be able to start to untangle your thoughts from those that are societal, familial, or cultural expectations. If you, for instance, wrote that "Divorce is bad because no one in my family gets divorced," to the question about what divorce means to you, I ask you to dig deeper. Ask yourself how you feel about that as a familial expectation. Can it be okay for you to break the family tradition? If not, why not?

Divorce can bring with it shame, feelings of failure, disappointment, and guilt. The thoughts, "There is something wrong with me," "I'm not good enough to be married," or "I can't get anything right," can percolate up when we face divorce. We brutally compare ourselves to others who appear to have happy marriages. This is like comparing apples to suitcases. There is no comparison. It is a good way to beat ourselves up and reaffirm the negative thoughts I just mentioned.

When I got divorced, I believed there must be something irretrievably wrong with me if I couldn't make a marriage work. I held onto this thought after my divorce even knowing consciously that what I wanted in a marriage was never going to come to fruition with a man who was solely attracted to men. These deep undermining thoughts can talk us out of what we say we want in our lives. Only if we listen to them, however.

EXERCISE

Make a list in your journal of all of your thoughts about divorce. Start with these sentence completions below. Use each one as often as you can. Keep writing until there are no further thoughts on divorce.

Divorce is_____

_____

Being divorced means that_____

_____

As a divorced person, I am_____

_____

What happens to divorced people is_____

_____

The worst thing about divorce is_____

_____

The best thing about divorce is_____

_____

These exercises should help you to identify the limiting thoughts you had both about marriage and about divorce. We will talk about how to change them later in this chapter.

Failure

Most of us detest the word "failure" and to wholeheartedly apply it to any part of our lives feels totally wrong. Why do we think that? Why have such a negative connotation to something that is the backbone of many successes? You may have heard Michael Jordan talk about how often he had to fail to become the best basketball player. Many entrepreneurs write about how many companies they headed were dismal failures before they went on to become multi-millionaires. Well-known examples are Oprah and Steve Jobs. Why do we think it should be different with marriage? Could it be because we have an expectation that it is a once-in-a-lifetime occurrence that we must get right the first time? If that is so, what training and preparation did we receive to do it right in one try? Each of Michael Jordan's failures taught him something that he then used to move on to be the brilliant player that he was.

If our lessons on how to have a successful marriage came from watching our parents, how is that applicable? If they had a great marriage, that is cause for celebration for them but in no way is indicative that you will be able to do the same thing. You likely learned some relationship skills from them that will apply and be helpful. When those hormones kick in, they don't take these skills into account when they tell you, "That is the One!" Some of us bring great relationship skills into a marriage with the wrong person. We work hard to try to make it work, use every skill we have, but it doesn't. Divorce happens. This is a good failure, in my opinion. The opportunity here is to stop "casting pearls before swine," and use your skills where they will work.

What if the opposite was true for you? Your parents had a sucky marriage or even ended up divorced. Or you were raised by a single parent, who may or may not have had a partner. What did you learn from them about how to make a marriage work? Children learn most from what they see modeled and not from what is told to them. If this was your family situation, what did you see modeled about marriage?

My parents had what I'd call a "dysfunctional marriage." There was infidelity, substance abuse, and verbal abuse. I have to say honestly that I went into marriage totally ignorant of what it might take of me to make it successful. There wasn't even anyone I could ask to get knowledgeable advice. This is an example of a good, and in fact, quite predictable failure.

Failure is a word to make friends with, not just in relation to your divorce but for life. Failure does not have to mean that you stop, curl up, and never move forward. One of my favorite poems that applies to this is called *Autobiography in Five Chapters by Portia Nelson.* I offer it here.

I.

I walk down the street.

There is a deep hole in the sidewalk

I fall in.

I am lost...

I am hopeless.

It isn't my fault.

It takes forever to find a way out.

II.

I walk down the same street.

There is a deep hole in the sidewalk.

I pretend I don't see it.

I fall in again.

I can't believe I'm in the same place.

But it isn't my fault.

It still takes a long time to get out.

III.

I walk down the same street.

There is a deep hole in the sidewalk.

I see it is there.

I still fall in... it's a habit

My eyes are open; I know where I am;

It is my fault.

I get out immediately.

IV.

I walk down the same street.

There is a deep hole in the sidewalk.

I walk around it.

V.

I walk down another street.

If you use this book, the practices in it, and your developing awareness about yourself and marriage, it will help you to start to either walk around the same-old-same-old relationship problems or choose an entirely different street to walk down.

Being Single

Have you noticed how often on various application forms that we fill out through our lives we are asked if we are Single/Never Married, Married, Divorced, or Widowed? Our identity is defined, on these applications, in relationship to marriage. I would posit that this is a subtle way that we are forced to continue to define ourselves. Here's what I mean by this.

What difference does it make to anyone (except maybe the IRS or someone I want to date) what my marital status is? Insurance companies like to know because there are statistics that marriage helps parts of the populations live longer. But why are we even asked this so often? It is not only on application forms. We ask this of each other as identifying information in order to categorize each other.

Whose business is it anyway? I believe that this is one of the ways in which we relentlessly push each other to define ourselves according to imposed norms. This question arose for me because I wanted to know when I get to be Single again after Divorced? Or do I? If I don't, why not? Do I have to continue to answer the question, "Are you married?" with "No, I'm divorced," for the rest of my life? Or until I get remarried? Given all the judgments we have on divorce, this can also be a not-so-subtle-push to get out of that state ASAP. The last thing I want when I introduce myself to others is to start with something that shows my failure. One of my clients was furious when her ex listed himself on a dating site as Single. "It is as if our marriage never existed!" she wailed. We spent time working on her sense of herself until *she* could comfortably fit into the identity of Single.

How you hold yourself after your marriage ends and how you make meaning of these different marital statuses can affect your sense of identity and worth as a person. I was at a workshop with a room full of women years after my divorce. The workshop leader gave a lecture on the social statuses of women. Her teaching was that the women in our culture who we nominate as having the highest status are women who are married with children. The women we see at the bottom of the status hierarchy are women who never married and have no children. This is a gruesome way to think about ourselves as women, especially if you are single and have no intention to get married and have children. To be seen as less-than for making that life choice is brutal and oppressive. We, as women, hold this standard in place. Men surely play a role in it, but ask yourself, how often, when you were married, did you feel sorry for a woman who was not married or who was, but didn't have children? How often did you wonder about the women without children, why they didn't have them? Did you judge them for being childless? We have a difficult time accepting that not all women have paths that lead to marriage and/or children. What is your path? Do you know?

Part of what is mortifying when our status changes from Married to Divorced is that our actual social status also changes. We take a big step down in the eyes of others, in particular, women. Thankfully, this is changing as more and more young women choose happily to remain single and/or childless. This does not mean that the pressure on them to marry and have children is necessarily decreasing. There are just more of them to support each other in the face of it.

Women after divorce are also not jumping right into new marriages based on the need to regain their social status. Many of us discover that being single is fan-f'ing-tastic! It is when we get to this awareness that we can check the box that says "Single" with great joy and peace.

Whatever your goals are in relation to remarrying, my advice, which you can take or leave, is to take it very slowly. Re-examine your thoughts on marriage and being single. Discover for yourself where you limit yourself and be courageous enough to change.

Change Your Thoughts

To change your thoughts is the most powerful thing you can do to recover from your divorce and to move forward into a life you create consciously. I've had lots of teachers in this methodology and it continues to be a necessary everyday practice. Those old, self-limiting, "I am a failure" thoughts can sneak up on you at any time. They become habitual voices in our heads. I practice telling them, when I'm in a strong place, "Thank you for sharing but I don't need to hear that right now," or when I'm more stressed by what they are telling me, "SHUT UP!"

Michael Bernard Beckwith, who is the founder of the Agape Church in Los Angeles, tells us to "Be happy now!" as did Meyer Baba, if you remember his teachings. How to do that when your heart is broken and the tears are ever present or when you are full of rage and disappointment, wanting just to hurt your former partner, is the $64,000 question.

Your emotions cannot be denied. They tell you that you are alive. Right now you hurt. Unlike the pain that comes from say, a broken bone, emotional pain can be transformed instantly. When you become more expert at this, you actually may discover that the pain of a broken bone can also be transformed but let's start with your broken heart.

As you journaled about marriage and divorce, you captured some of the thoughts and beliefs about yourself that you are walking around with every day, probably all day long. How many of them make you feel joyful? Or even at peace? When you wrote them down, which ones caused you to feel emotions other than happiness? Take note of these. These are the ones that need to be transformed.

Have you heard the expression that thought is creative? This means my thoughts create results in my life. Your thoughts create results in yours. You are the thinker who creates.

If I went into my marriage with deeply held thoughts, based on my lived experience that marriages don't last, are dysfunctional and hurtful whether or not the people in them love each other, what do you think the result would be in my life? I did think this. I also believed that I could do it differently without rooting out this deeply held belief. I thought that I just had to take different actions and I would have a functional, lasting marriage. Wrong!

Here's the sticky wicket. If our thoughts are not in alignment with our actions, we don't get the prize. Here's another example. Think of Venus Williams. She is brilliant at the game of tennis. What if, however, she had a deeply held belief that she couldn't win? Do you think for a minute that she would be where she is today? Muhammad Ali demonstrated this the best when he was boxing by continually affirming to himself and the world that he was the greatest. He became that. Here is a quote from Reverend Michael:

Creation is always happening. Every time an individual has a thought, or a prolonged, chronic way of thinking, they're in the creation process.

Something is going to manifest out of those thoughts.

– Michael Bernard Beckwith

I want to be really clear that this is not about blame. It is not one further thing that you did wrong. We don't want to go to, "Oh, because I had thoughts that marriage doesn't work, I screwed up my marriage." Please do not go there!! That is another ego-driven, beat-yourself-up trap that will not aid in your healing. Instead, look at the results in your life; figure out what thoughts created them; and be grateful. You are on a path of discovery and there are no accidents or mistakes on this path. It is your path, filled with your lessons, no one else's. Part of the process of choosing to alter the path, widen it – or perhaps, change directions entirely – is to unearth the thoughts that keep us stuck. It is a process I invite you to trust.

Remember when I said that what you focus on expands? This doesn't just mean consciously. All of those thoughts that are unconscious, or that we don't really pay attention to, expand in our reality each moment. They create results for us that are easy to see, if we look.

EXERCISES

New Thoughts

What are you focusing on right now? Which of your thoughts that you listed in the previous exercises are you willing to change, transform, reframe, or see differently? Pick at least one, get that journal, and let's do it. Here's how. Look at the thought and ask yourself these questions:

✓ How does this thought make me feel?

✓ Is this thought serving me? If it is, how is it serving me?

✓ Does this thought help me to heal from my divorce?

✓ What payoff am I getting from continuing to believe that this thought is true?

✓ What would it be like for me if this thought was not true?

✓ What other thought could I choose to replace it?

Write that new thought and any others that come to mind in your journal.

Practice replacing the old thought with the new thought every time the old one comes into your conscious awareness. You can do it as I do by saying, "Thank you, but I choose to believe *this* today," or "Shut up! I believe this." Do whatever works to chase the old thought away and replace it with one that helps you feel stronger and inspired.

If you just read through this chapter and did not do the journaling exercises, I suggest you go back and do them as your exercise. The exercise below won't make much sense if you haven't done the preparatory work.

In the next chapter, we will continue to examine your thoughts and how they impact the fears you may have about the future.

Everywhere a Sign

Make a colorful sign with each of your new thoughts. Place them where you will see them daily. Use them as a screensaver on your computer. Find as many ways as possible to bring them to your conscious awareness all day long.

Practice saying "My failures make me great!" and "Every time I fail, I get better at life."

(Optional: Listen to Bobby McFerrin or Bob Marley sing, *"Don't Worry Be Happy."*)

Chapter Ten

LOVE, FEAR, AND LESSONS

Love is what we are born with.
Fear is what we learn.
The spiritual journey is the unlearning of fear
and prejudices and the acceptance of love back
in our hearts. Love is the essential reality and
our purpose on earth.
To be consciously aware of it, to experience
love in ourselves and others,
is the meaning of life. Meaning does not lie in
things. Meaning lies in us.
– Marianne Williamson

We looked at the thoughts you had related to marriage, divorce, being single, and failure. Let's spend time looking at your fears of the future to see if there are other thoughts you might want to root out and transform. We will examine the lessons from your marriage and I will offer a practice to manage stress.

Divorce is an opportunity for huge transformation and to confront fears that have been held in abeyance. As I said earlier, one of the reasons I married stemmed from my fear of being alone. How would my life have been different if I had not been ruled by that fear? It doesn't matter where or how I learned that fear only that I, later, after my divorce, made a committed effort to confront it and see being alone differently. The goal of this chapter is to help you assess your fears and choose to allow yourself to love and accept them.

We spend our lives running from, medicating, denying, and avoiding our fears. None of these techniques usually work other than temporarily. Sure, it is uncomfortable to feel that churning in your stomach or tightness in your chest. When we face and accept our fears, they lose their power over us. Our task is to learn to lean into them. Welcome them. Welcome their guidance. If we stay in the present moment with them instead of spinning off with all kinds of dramatic stories, they tend to dissipate. We then have an opening for creative freedom.

Fear

Have you heard that depression happens when we focus on the past and anxiety when we focus on the future? The depression that can follow a divorce is often rooted in revisiting all the mistakes; all the things that went wrong; or all the things that we now lack that were present in the past. The anxiety that can come hand in hand with the depression comes out of our worry about all the things that are changing. We feel we have no control over them and oftentimes fear that our worst-case scenario is about to come true. This fear can keep us up nights; push us to make precipitous decisions; cause us to eat too much or not at all; and in many other ways, drive us crazy.

We worry that we will be homeless. We worry we won't be able to support ourselves or our children. We worry we will never find another partner. We worry the next partner we find will be just like the one we left and another failure. We worry that we will die alone. We worry about whether or not we will ever have sex again. We worry that we won't want to have sex ever again. We worry about our safety in the world, especially as a single woman. We worry about our partner finding a mate before we do. This is the short list. There are most likely hundreds of detailed worries and fears that shriek through your mind every day.

There is a good side to fear and anxiety, compared to depression. While depression saps our energy and prevents us from taking any actions, anxiety gives us energy. We may feel revved up and ready to go all the time. A study in 1985 by Shipman & Shipman showed that a small amount of anxiety helps us to be better test-takers. At the same time, too much of it and we fail the test miserably and may not even be able to stay in the classroom. In other words, anxiety can be a great motivator or can cripple us.

In general, what is the level of your anxiety at this moment? We are only able to answer this for the moment we are in because our feelings change throughout the day like the weather. On a scale of 1 – 10, with 1 being totally calm and 10 being massively worried or anxious, where are you right now? Use this scale throughout the day to check in with yourself. When your anxiety is at a 10, there are steps you might want to take to bring it down.

One of the ways you can bring yourself back to a place of greater peace is to use grounding exercises. These fantastic practices were designed for people who have experienced forms of trauma but also work well for your run-of-the-mill anxiety. Below is a grounding practice you can use anywhere, at any time. I taught this practice to a client in person during a session. She was so stressed about the plan we had just made together to take the bus alone to an unknown location that her hands started shaking. Her eyes were darting around like she wanted to run out of the session. As I guided her through the practice of becoming grounded, her breathing slowed and her eyes refocused. We were able to readjust her plan to take smaller steps and to include this practice as needed before each step she took. The following week she reported proudly that she had not only ridden the bus twice alone but she had used grounding to help her during it.

Grounding

Grounding brings you back into the here and now. Use it when you feel anxiety that clouds your thinking and causes you to breathe too fast. Use it any time you want to bring yourself fully into the present moment.

You can sit, stand, or lie down. It can be done indoors or outdoors but may be less distracting and feel safer if you are inside. What you do is notice where you are in great detail. Start by doing the scaling exercise to see what level your anxiety is to start. Is it a 3 or a 9?

Take three deep, slow breaths with your eyes open.

Look around you with attention.

Notice what is to the right of you, to the left of you, behind you, above you, and in front of you. Swivel your head around and let your eyes rotate around the room. Look at and notice everything around you for a full minute. Take your time.

Notice the temperature in the room. Is it hot? Cold?

Notice the floor under your feet. What color is it? What is its texture? How does it sound when you move your feet? What do your feet feel like in your shoes as they rub against it?

Notice the chair you are sitting in. What color is it? What is it made out of? Feel the arms or seat with your fingers. What does it feel like? How does it feel against your back? Under your butt? Take your time to notice the details.

Notice the walls in the room. What color are they? What is their texture? Notice how they meet the ceiling. Notice how they meet the floor. Are there gaps? If there are patterns, notice them.

Place your hands palm down on the tops of your thighs. What does that feel like? Feel the texture of your clothing. Rub your palms slowly up and down on the tops of your thighs. Notice how your hands feel. Notice how your thighs feel.

Scale the anxiety again. Has it come down? If not, continue to choose items in the room to notice with this level of focus and detail. Repeat until you know that you are safe and the anxiety is in a more manageable range.

Once you are in the 1–3 range, we can continue on to the lessons you are learning or have learned from your marriage and divorce.

When we use grounding, we bring ourselves into the present moment. The noticing helps the survival part of the brain recognize that no danger exists right now so it can relax and let you relax.

Lessons

I love the concept that whatever happens in your life is either about love or it is a lesson to help you expand your ability to love. In other words, it's either love or it's a lesson.

Each aspect of your marriage or divorce that causes you pain right now is a lesson. This is the opportunity to learn it. I have seen over and over in my own and my clients' lives that when we don't take advantage of the lesson the first time, it comes around again and again until we learn it.

Here's a lesson from my own life related to the struggles in my marriage. Alcoholism was a recurring theme in my family home. No surprise then that I would choose to marry an alcoholic. I was blind to it in my family. Likewise, when I got married, I was blind to that reality. As my eyes were opened to the family issue, I suddenly saw that my husband had the disease of alcoholism. As a result, I became a grateful member of the Al-Anon family groups and practiced the Twelve Steps of recovery from this perspective. Once I was divorced, single, and not living with an alcoholic, I decided I no longer needed to be in active recovery and stopped my daily practices. You may be able to guess who my next relationship was with. A very active alcoholic. The only difference between him and my ex was that he was a happy drunk not a mean one. I had not, you see, fully gotten the lesson.

The person or issue in your life right now that is the most aggravating to you is your current teacher, your guru. Only you can figure out what you need to learn. Only you can keep asking the question, "What am I *really* upset about?" when you think about them. Whatever that thing is, is the lesson. What do you need to learn from it?

My own fear of homelessness led me to work with people who were struggling with homelessness. That work helped me to banish that fear as I made friends with people who were homeless. I saw how easily it could be me and at the same time had great compassion for their situations. When I was able to accept them as just like me, instead of as a scary *other*, the fear abated. The lesson is to lean into whatever the fears are; accept them instead of fighting against them; and make friends with them. They may be a portal to a whole new experience that you can't even imagine.

Think about times in your life that you were most worried or fearful. What decisions did you make about how you were going to proceed in your life? Did these decisions move your life forward in a way that you now feel is productive or did they hold you back? We can make decisions coming out of a fear-based situation that stop us in our tracks for years to come. My mother, after her divorce, told me that she was never going to love again because it hurt too much when it ended. She never kept pets for the same reason. She didn't want to feel the pain when they died. This was her method of coping with her fear of pain. What is yours? Are you limiting yourself? Are you moving forward despite your fears? I call that "fearing forward." Others call it leaning into your fear. Whatever you want to call it, it is your choice. You can take the steps you need to take while your knees are knocking and your hands are sweating or stay put, where it is comfortable and safe. Either will produce results. The question is: Which result do you want?

Love is not safe, although we want it to be. Love is not secure, although we want to believe it is. Love is not unchanging, although we take vows as if that were true. If you want to invite new love into your life, you must be willing to live on the edge at all times, knowing that there is no safety, security, or stability in it, in and of itself. Does that mean we can't create lives that feel safe, secure, and stable? Of course not, but it is a lie we tell ourselves in order to get through the day.

I live in California. Many of my East Coast friends think I'm crazy to live somewhere with "all those earthquakes." I wake up every morning convinced that I am safe and that the earth is not going to crack under my feet. But it could at any moment. Because of my deep love for my life here, I choose not to focus on that as my reality.

In the next chapter, we will see how you can manifest the life you want. Before that though, let's examine some of these fears and lessons.

EXERCISE

Looking at the fears and worries that came up for you as you read this chapter, write in your journal what you learned from each of these life experiences. If your fear or anxiety starts to go up as you journal about these events, use the grounding exercise.

Practice the grounding exercise when you are not anxious. This will allow you to learn how to do it so it will be easier and more available when you do need it.

(Optional: Here's a song for this chapter: *The Rose* by Bette Midler. Listen to it turned up loud and sing along.)

Chapter Eleven

MANIFEST AND GET WHAT YOU WANT

Desire, ask, believe, receive.
– Stella Terrill Mann

I don't know what you're up against,
I don't know what you're facing.
But here's what I do know:
You've got something special, you've got
greatness in you,
and I know it's possible that you can
live your dream.
– Les Brown

We looked at fears and lessons in the last chapter. Let's have some fun now and begin to create anew. Let's look at ways to manifest your vision of what you want. First, I want to talk about getting the help and support that you want and need because we never have to do it all on our own.

Ask for Help

When we divorce, rifts occur from friends, family members, and other natural supports. They also can occur between us and paid supports. We may not want to use the same accountant as our ex or the same auto mechanic. We may want to change grocery stores, banks, or dry cleaners. There are lots of little decisions like this. You can use the finger-in-the-circle method to help you make the decisions about who you want to stay connected to. What about when there are too many things to take care of at once? You may have had a shared workload. Now it is all on you. An important question to answer for yourself is, "Who can I ask for help?" Who can you call when you just need to vent? Who can you ask to come over and fix your thermostat when it is freezing out and the heat won't go on? Who can you call to pick you up at the airport after a long flight? Who can you ask to take care of your dogs or cats when you travel? Who can you ask to drive you to work when your car is in the shop? I could go on for a whole chapter.

You need supporters. You need people in your life for all kinds of things. Some you will need to pay. Many will be happy just to help you out. Are you open to receive this support? That is the crucial question. If you are steeped in shame and feeling like you have to pull it all together by yourself, this is going to take a long time and be pretty painful. If you have supporters already, use them and make sure to appreciate them extensively. If you currently don't have enough support, you can use the manifestation practice below to bring these people into your life in an energetic way. You can also practice asking. Ask anyone you know, who you think might be good at a particular thing, if they will help you with it. If you are open to receive, you will be amazed at your results. Asking for help is another practice that the more you do it, the better you get at it – the easier it will become for you to receive.

You have to be willing to accept "No" for an answer and not let it dissuade you from asking someone else. If you ask ten people for support or help and three agree, you are a rock star at this. Don't keep a tally, though. Just keep asking for what you need from actual people and, as we will see in the practices below, from God or the Universe, as well.

Manifestation

There are multiple ways to manifest what you want in your life. I am going to teach you the two that have been most powerful in mine. The first one is a form of visualization. As a visual artist, I am very attracted to and motivated by images. One of my most highly developed senses is my vision. To manifest things in my life, I use this sense to bring into being what I want to see. This will work for you whether or not you are an artist. No special art skills are necessary.

Earlier in the Exercises, you made a collage with you in the center to help you envision characteristics that you have and/ or want to own and strengthen. Here we are going to create a collage called a Vision Board to call forth the actual things and realities you want in your life. I will describe how to do it and you will make one for yourself.

This has been so overwhelmingly successful in my own life that I use it sparingly. I have had the experience multiple times of manifesting exactly what I put on my Boards. When I was looking for someone to date, I made a Vision Board in which I pasted images of a man who I thought was totally gorgeous. I thought I would love to date someone like him. I found his photo in a fashion magazine. It was only a matter of months before I met this exact same man on a bus in New

York City and started dating him. I didn't meet someone who looked like him. I met him.

Years later, I made a board on which I pasted an image of a young woman hiking in the Colorado mountains. I chose that image because I wanted to take a trip to Colorado and go hiking. In a short time, I had a new roommate who was a hiker from Colorado, who looked like the woman on the Vision Board. In neither of these instances did I see what had happened right away. With the man I met, I had put the board up in my bedroom but was not consciously looking at it every day, so I didn't notice that he was the same man. For my roommate, I still had the board up in my living room while she was living with me, and neither one of us noticed that it looked like her. It was only when I took the time later to look carefully at all the items on my board to see what I had manifested that I saw that I had gotten exactly and quite specifically what I had asked for.

I offer these stories to prompt you to be precise in both the images and words that you choose. I learned to be open to how the things showed up in my life, too. It is not always how I thought I wanted them to. I have many, many stories about how the different Vision Boards I made manifested things and people in my life, as I have been using this tool for 30 years. Not only are they fun to make, but they work.

How to Make a Vision Board

You will need some supplies to make a board. Start by gathering your supplies. Here is the list:

- ✓ A photo of you that you like
- ✓ Magazines with colorful words and photos

✓ An illustration board. This can be as large or small as you want. The larger the better, so you can choose large images and can see them from across the room.

✓ A glue stick

✓ Scissors

Set aside a few hours to make your board. Listen to some inspiring music while you make it. This is an enjoyable practice to do with a friend who supports your vision and wants to make their own board.

Flip through the magazines quickly, tear out any images or words that strike you as representing what you want. For instance, if you want a new Tesla, find a great photo of a Tesla as well as the words, "My," "New," and "Car." You are going to use not only images but also words describing what the image is that affirms it. Like I described in my story, if you don't name it as *your* new car, you may just find yourself noticing that your neighbor has the exact car that you want. You called the car into your life but not exactly as you wanted.

You can pull out images and words related to a lot of different areas of your life or you can make a separate vision board for each. For instance, if you want to travel you could make one that shows all of the places you want to go. It is best to have a goal for your board before you start finding pictures to help you focus. If you get stuck and just can't find a photo of the exact Tesla you want, you can use Google images to find one and print it out. Color images work most powerfully, so print in color if you can.

It is easy to find words like, "You can," and "the best," in magazines. Cut out big, bold, and positive statements about yourself and your life.

You can build your board a little at a time or you can pull out all the images and words that you can find and then place them in a pleasing arrangement. This is your vision board. No one else has to like it or even see it. Please don't let the "I can't make art. I'm not an artist," gremlins have any space in your mind. Have fun and make something that you enjoy looking at.

When you are ready to build it, put your own image in the center and surround yourself with all of the things that you want to call into your life. You can tack them down using your glue stick and then rearrange them until you get them in an arrangement you like. Once you have a vision board that inspires you, glue everything in place.

There are a couple of additional things to add to your board. I recommend having an image that represents God, Spirit, or the Universe. I have used images of the sun, an Om sign, or a picture of a bird. Whatever works for you. A phrase that you can type, print, and glue on is, "This or something better now manifests for me with good to all concerned." It is a wonderful affirmation for all of the positive changes you want.

Once you have all of your words and images glued on around the photo of yourself, choose a spot in your home where you can see it often and regularly. These images and words will work on your creative mind whether you sit and meditate on them or not, as long as they are visible to you. I keep my vision boards private because I do not want any additional energy from friends or family members to interrupt or disturb my manifestation process.

Now let's talk about Affirmative Prayer as a manifestation practice.

Affirmative Prayer

Regardless of your religious or spiritual beliefs, this is a form of prayer, also called spiritual treatment that will work if you use it. It is taught by various non-denominational churches, such as Unity and the Church of Religious Science. The purpose of this treatment is to state clearly, and as often as possible, what you want in your life. Using this prayer is a way to claim it for yourself. If, as I believe, all change starts in the mind first, then we have to make up our minds about what we want, visualize it, and state it to ourselves and to the Universe or God. There are five steps in this form of prayer. What I love about it is that everyone can create their own version, in their own words, so that it truly resonates with them. My prayers will be different from yours. I will share one after I describe to you the steps to creating your own.

The first step is Recognition. In this step we recognize God, Spirit, Universal Mind, Nature, or whatever you call It. It is an acknowledgement of the Infinite and our recognition of that. It might sound like this: "There is only One Life. That Life is God. That Life is whole, perfect, and complete."

The second step is Unification. Here we state our acknowledgement that we are a part of God, Spirit, or this Infinite Intelligence. We are an individual expression of the Divine and you are a part of the Divine Whole. Here I would say something like, "That Life is my life now."

The third step is Declaration. This is where I affirm what I want to affirm in my life. By this I mean, what do I want to say and pray to be true in my life, even though it may not be totally that way at the moment of my prayer. This is not about praying to be a multimillionaire if you are working at a fast food restaurant. Instead, you would affirm that your prosperity is increasing exponentially to allow God to bring it in any number of ways. If my prayer is for perfect health even though my current reality is that I am struggling with some health issues, my Declaration would be, "I, Marsha Vaughn, declare that I have perfect, radiant health; that all my physical systems are working in harmony with each other and I feel great!" One difference between this process and your vision board is that here you are being more general and not as specific in your desires. The reason for this is to allow God to bring gifts in unexpected ways.

The fourth step is Thanksgiving. You already know how I feel about giving thanks. This is a way to work it into every prayer you say. You have an opportunity here to celebrate regularly all of the gifts you receive or have. It can change our reality when we start to name these everyday things and see how blessed our lives actually are. This step begins by affirming that we know the Truth. In this philosophy, the Truth is that all things come from and are a part of God, Spirit, or the Universal Mind. There is no separation. Nothing is outside of this. You start with, "I give thanks for knowing the Truth." You can follow that with all of the things you want to give thanks for at that moment. I always start by giving thanks for, "all the blessings in my life." Then I go on to list things like my dogs, my family, my health, etc.

The final and fifth step is Release. This is where we let go and let God. We let God take over making our prayer a reality.

We let go of trying to control and make things happen. Instead we allow them to unfold, in God's time and with Divine direction. That could sound like, "I now release my word to the Divine Activity of the Law, knowing as I do, that God always says, 'Yes!'" What is meant by the Divine Activity of the Law is, to put it very simply, that our thought creates results, whether we are conscious of them or not.

You can end and seal the prayer with, "Amen," "Ashe" or "And so it is."

Here is an affirmative prayer that I wrote for the purpose of writing this book.

My Prayer

There is only one Life. That Life is God. That Life is my life now.

I, Marsha Vaughn, speak my word for a successful book launch. My life as an author is divinely guided, prospers me and others, and brings peace and joy to me daily. It is a source of abundance and support.

I give thanks for knowing the Truth. I give thanks for all the blessings in my life. I give thanks for my book coach, my supportive friends, my computer and internet connection, my ability to type, all the authors I have met, my dogs, my health, my vision, and my ongoing and ever-increasing prosperity.

I release my word into the Divine Activity of the Law knowing that God has got my back. God wants me to prosper and spread my knowledge widely. I let go and I let God.

And so it is. Amen.

EXERCISE

Create a vision board related to whatever area of your life is calling most loudly for something new. Follow the steps above to make it.

Your second exercise is to create your own Affirmative Prayer. Once you have it in a form that you like, write it down to carry with you and read it throughout the day. If you learn the five steps to create a prayer, you can create new ones on the spot. As I mentioned, Reverend E., who taught me how to do this, says, "Pray without ceasing." Affirm what you want often and always. Trust God, let go, and watch it unfold.

(Optional: Listen to music that brings into mind your most beautiful vision for your life. I like Ricky Byars Beckwith, *Spirit of God Is upon Me.*)

Chapter Twelve
WHAT WILL KEEP
YOU STUCK

You have been given the keys.
It is now your job to take them,
unlock your cage, and set yourself free.
– Angela E. Lauria

If you don't go after what you want,
you'll never have it.
If you don't ask, the answer is always no.
If you don't step forward, you're always
in the same place.
– Nora Roberts

First, I want to congratulate you on getting this far. If you have read this much, you have a strong desire to recover from your divorce. If you integrated the practices in each chapter into your life and use them daily, that tells me that you are clearly committed to your rapid recovery from this loss. If you have read along and thought, "Sounds good. I'll do it later," you are like most of us. Most people who buy self-help books like this one will read them, maybe take some notes or get excited about some of the ideas. Life continues to call us, and we forget about them. We don't review our notes or put into practice any of the ideas. I speak from personal experience here.

In my work as a therapist, I worked for most of my career with traumatized people. People who had suffered from child abuse, sexual assault, homelessness, incarceration – you name it. This type of work wears on you. It is easy to start to feel burnt out and just not care anymore. One of the best books I have read and which I recommend to others regularly on how to care for yourself when you are doing this type of work is, *"Trauma Stewardship: An Everyday Guide to Caring for Self While Caring for Others* by Laura van Dernoot Lipsky. I read about how others' trauma impacted me and, towards the end, lots of helpful suggestions on what I could do to change my relationship to the trauma work I was doing so I wouldn't burn out. They all sounded great. Did I do them? Nope. Not a one. I thought I was desperate to find a solution to how my work was impacting me. It was making me miserable, stressed, overweight, and numb. You would have thought I would have gotten right to it and taken all that good advice. You would have been wrong. I still use this book as my guide to understand the impact of trauma on caregivers. It is the best! I needed a different way though to actually do the things that were recommended to me. Reading a book in the comfort of my bed didn't push me hard enough. What I wanted at the time was to have a personal relationship with Laura van Dernoot Lipsky, so she could teach me in person what I needed to know. She was busy speaking around the country. I didn't have the courage to contact her and ask her for that.

How this related to my divorce is that a few months after my divorce, it became obvious to me that I needed help. I wanted help to manage the level of disappointment and the baffling new questions I was facing about who I was and what I wanted for my life. Sitting in my big, comfortable chair with my cats, binge-watching *Law & Order, SVU,* and eating pasta was not helping. I wasn't sleeping well. I cried a lot. My thinking felt fuzzy all the time. I was isolating. I had the classic symptoms of depression, which, being a therapist, you'd think I would have recognized immediately. I didn't. I bought Pema Chodron's book, *When Things Fall Apart,* and read it every day. I learned to meditate. I filled dozens of journals. I took dance classes to get moving. I did a lot of stuff on my own. Don't get me wrong. Each element helped incrementally. It was a heavy lift, however, to do alone. Each thing, in and of itself, did a little to help me overcome my ever-present self-doubts. When it all started to come together was when I reached out to a therapist to help me through this dark time. I also turned to a friend who was a coach.

Because of the strong feelings of failure that can accompany divorce, it might be a terrifying thing to think about taking chances in any area of your life. "What if I fail at that?" Taking a step in a totally new direction can feel like the most insane thing to do. We want to overcome both these feelings of self-doubt and failure and the accompanying thoughts that go with them. Where do we start? We start with the thought. If you sit around thinking, as I did, "Change is scary and I might get hurt again," you will sit around feeling scared and not doing anything to make the changes that you believe you want desperately. We have to change those thoughts first.

Over time, I have gotten better at ferreting out the thoughts that are causing me pain. This is another thing that requires practice over and over again before you become an expert at it. Both my therapist and my coach were able to help me with different parts when I got stuck. I needed someone else to ask me, "What is it you are thinking about that?" or a series of questions to help me see where I was stuck and causing my own pain.

Another reason we stay stuck is because we keep doing the same things over and over and expecting a different result. You know that this is often cited as a definition of insanity. We have a hard time seeing that we are repeating ourselves in thoughts and actions. Someone else can see it more readily. If your response to feeling like you have failed at something is to retreat and hide, as mine was, you will be doing that now. If your response is to get out there and conquer some new challenge to overcome that awful feeling of failure and to prove to the world that you are not one, you will do that. That might produce a more positive result than hiding does. At the same time, it could as likely send you into situations that are not the most supportive for you if you are being driven by fear and self-doubt rather than by your inner spiritual compass. This is how people end up marrying the same person over again a few months after getting divorced.

These habitual responses to situations take effort to change. First you have to know you are doing the same thing again. That means you have to be aware of it. You have to accept that about yourself and own it. Then you can take actions to change it. Most of the practices in this book are to further your awareness of yourself, to help you accept yourself, and to give you the tools to take the actions needed to make the changes that you want.

Why don't we use the tools that we are given? If you are like me, you might try for a bit and if you don't get an immediate result, you give up. "Oh, I tried that! It doesn't work for me." If only I had $100 for every time I've heard a client say that! We do try. Once. Maybe if we are really committed, we try a few times. When the new activity or practice is not a magic bullet and doesn't produce an immediate result, we give up. You may be feeling this way already about the practices I've recommended that you have tried a couple of times.

There is a big difference between "trying" and "doing." We use the word "try" as a back door. It communicates that I want this, but I just might go out the back door if it doesn't give me what I want fast enough. We check out and abandon it. I like to demonstrate this difference to clients by showing them how it works. While remaining seated in a chair, I say, "Here is me trying to get up." I don't move. Then I say, "Here is me getting up." I get up out of the chair. This can bring up some anger for sure. It can feel like I am saying you aren't *trying* hard enough. That is so totally not the point. The point is that you will never achieve your dreams by trying. You will accomplish them if you take the necessary steps. If you get up out of the chair and take the next right step. If you practice, practice, practice, and practice some more until you are a master. That is where the results show up.

An ongoing challenge to creating a life that we love out of the ashes of our previous life is how hard it all feels. Who wants to do things that feel hard? Especially when everything hurts. I have to tell you the truth. It is not for the faint-hearted. You have the courage to have come this far. You took the step to leave a life that didn't work for you. As you take the next steps into a life that does, know that at times it will seem like it is getting much worse before it gets better. All those expressions about it being darkest before the dawn are true. As we break old habits, learn new ways of living and being, and challenge our old, not useful thoughts, they will fight back.

In family systems theory, the analogy of a hanging mobile is used to describe this. If one person in a family changes, it is like one piece of the mobile moves. This causes all of the pieces of the mobile to move around but eventually they settle back into the same arrangement, in balance. Family systems do not encourage change usually. In our individual lives, if we change one area, it is like moving a piece of our inner mobile. The habitual ways our brain and life have worked together to keep us in this state of balance are threatened. We experience a little movement but eventually want to settle back into the same old, same old. When we keep going, keep moving, and keep changing, we have a chance to disrupt that unhealthy balance and create a new one. This takes commitment and fortitude.

Does this sound like a lot of work? It is. There is no magic bullet. If there were, would you really want to use it anyway? Much of the fantastic feelings and results we get in life come from the effort we put into things. When we challenge ourselves right up to the edge of our comfort zone and then succeed at something, that is the moment when we jump and scream with joy and amazement. It is overcoming all of the obstacles both internal and external that gives us such a rush.

I learned about the value of having a coach from running marathons – which oddly enough is similar to recovering from divorce. Anything that requires focus, attention, and the development of new skills is much easier to learn and become successful at if we have a coach. I started running marathons in my 40s with no past running experience. I say now that it was the main thing that prevented me from killing my husband. Running is one of the best ways to move energy, especially anger.

Because I had coaches who had run many marathons who told me what to expect and how to get through it, I was able to finish three of them. I read books on marathon running and learned a lot that way. It was the person-to-person, in-the-moment support that I believe helped me achieve that goal. Similarly, with my divorce the support through the hard passes that I received from my therapist and my coach helped me to move into new and scary territory. I was guided through these areas with kindness and support. Is there someone who is supporting and coaching you in moving forward? Who is calling out from the sidelines that, "You can do it?" Do you have someone reminding you of how precious you are? Are they holding the space for you to succeed at the new things you are trying while at the same time loving you when you mess up, get confused, or give up?

If there isn't someone who comes to mind who can play this role for you, know that there is the right person for you, waiting to be of service in this way. When you are ready and willing to allow them in and receive their support, they will show up in your life. Use the Applied Kinesiology or muscle testing practice to test for who is right. Pay deep attention. When we are wounded in our relational heart as we are after divorce, it can hurt to let love and caring into it again. That is a necessary part of the healing process. However, who we let in is crucial. We don't want to keep picking the wrong ones over and over again. I knew that my therapist had lost her husband six months before I started to work with her. Not to divorce but to death. When I met her at a seminar, I knew she had a deep understanding of grief and loss from her very presence. She was who I wanted to hold my hand through my own grief and loss. Who do you want to hold yours?

You have listed who could help you with the more mundane tasks of your life already. The question here is who can help you with the deeper work? Who can guide you through whatever practices you choose to use; keep you on task with your goals; and call you on your blind spots? The exercise for this chapter is designed to help you figure that out. The same barriers that come up when we are asking for help with finding a new job are likely to come up and may be fiercer. Here are some thoughts to watch for and some ways to respond to them when they come up. I recommend responding to them out loud if you can. Talking back to our negative thoughts is a great way to make them go away. You also get to choose a positive thought instead and affirm it out loud.

Thought: "I can't ask for someone to do that!"

Response: "Yes you can and you deserve it!"

Thought: "I don't need *that* kind of help!"

Response: "Yes, I do. I need someone to listen and care about me."

Thought: "I'm just divorced, not crazy!"

Response: "It is a sign of health to ask people for help."

Thought: "If I can't handle this myself, I'm really a mess,"

Response: "Honey, you've been handling a lot. Can you let someone else bear some of it for a bit?"

Thought: "What would my parents/sibling/ex/(fill in the blank) say if they knew?"

Response: "What other people think of me is none of my business."

Thought: "Only losers need therapists or coaches."

Response: "Thanks for sharing and shut up!" I use this one when my negative thoughts start to get obnoxious and call me names.

These types of thoughts will slow your progress, keep you stuck, and prevent your deeper healing. If this is confusing or challenging, it can also be a practice that you could look for help learning to master.

One final thought before we look at who could be a helper for you on the path through the darkness. Neuroscience is teaching us so many incredible things about how our brains work; how we are controlled by our hormones; how we can continue to change and learn throughout our lives. I remind my clients that when they are upset, emotional, or stressed, this is absolutely never the time to make a decision or plan. The part of our brain, our pre-frontal cortex that is in charge of logical thinking, planning, and organizing among other things, goes offline when we are flooded with emotions. What comes online are the areas of the brain responsible for our survival. We go into survival thinking and will take actions that we would never take if we were in a calmer state, where our brain doesn't think we are about to die. I mention this because when we are in our survival brains, it is hard to know it. It feels real. The threats feel real. It often takes another person who is not in their survival brain to help us to calm down, take a breath, and not take any actions until we are at a steady and stable state. The woman who I mentioned hated her job went from being on the precipice of quitting it to realizing that she didn't want to do that at all during our coaching session on forgiveness. I also reminded her of this brain fact.

When my anxiety about my future raised its ugly head, this was the hardest thing to do. When I was panicked about being homeless, that was my brain attempting to keep me safe. Thankfully, I had several people, including the realtor I worked with, who were able to help me calm my panic and make decisions about my living situation using my logical brain instead of my survival brain. A crucial component in receiving support is to find people who help you keep your pre-frontal cortex functioning optimally and who can bring you back from the edge of disaster each time you find yourself there. I am not suggesting asking your friends or family members, "Can you help me keep my pre-frontal cortex operating functionally?" I am suggesting you find who can help you to "Keep Calm and Carry On." Let's use the exercise in this chapter to figure out who that might be.

EXERCISE

List all the qualities you would like in a supporter, therapist, or coach. Be specific. Who do you feel safe with when you are vulnerable? What is their gender, age, race, etc.? Draw yourself a picture in words of who they are. What characteristics do they have? Qualities that I recommend are that they are a good listener and they will always tell you the truth, even when it is uncomfortable. What else helps you to feel heard and understood?

What style do you want? For instance, I describe helpers as either crisp or squishy.

The crisp ones have a direct approach, are confrontational in a caring way, and are logical about the information they present. The squishy ones radiate feelings of warmth and concern so you feel like you are being emotionally embraced. They may be less directive, too. This is all on a continuum. Helpers who have a logical and crisp approach should also be emotionally warm. We all have our strong suits. Coaches are no exception. Find one who resonates with you.

Another area to investigate is whether you are a spiritual match, What kind of religious or spiritual practices do you want them to understand or know about? Or do you want to learn from them? Drawing on our connection to God can lead to powerful healing. It helps to speak the same language of faith.

Once you get a clear picture of what this person should be like, don't be surprised if they show up in your life. If you have questions about finding a either a therapist or a coach or want to share your successes with me and how the various practices have worked, I would love to hear from you.

In the next chapter we will put this together with everything else you have learned and create specific goals. I hope that one of them is to find the right helper.

Chapter Thirteen

YOUR NEW LIFE PLAN – LET'S DO THIS!

*Life is like playing a violin in public and
learning the instrument as one goes along.*
– Samuel Butler

Nothing can bring you peace but yourself.
– Ralph Waldo Emerson

*Great emergencies and crises show us
how much greater our vital resources are than
we had supposed.*
– William James

Okay, let's put it all together and make a plan for what is next. I am reminded of the old Yiddish saying "Mann tracht, un Gott lacht," which translates to "Man plans, and God laughs." Have you ever noticed that sometimes the best laid plans become a comedy of errors? That is what this expression means. I paraphrase this to clients as we are making plans. "Remember when you make a plan, God laughs," I say. They laugh uneasily, not quite wanting to believe this. We all want to make plans and have them work out exactly as written. We erroneously think we are in control when we do this. Sometimes they work out. Often they do not. Holding your plan lightly and with awareness of this helps to mitigate the possible anger and disappointment when plans go awry. When we are making a plan for our own self-improvement and recovery, it is vital that we hold this plan with intention but also lightly. Your Life Plan should never be a reason to beat yourself up. If you don't meet one of your objectives, as I will describe, that is not the time to add on more shame or judge yourself as even more of a failure.

If God is laughing at our plan, to me, that shows that God has a better plan; a bigger idea for me than I could imagine for myself. When I see botched plans in this light, it helps my little ego to let go of thinking that I am in control of all of the outcomes in my life. For someone who loves to feel in control as a way to manage my anxiety, this is a necessary step to letting go while feeling safe. I can Let Go and Let God, since I know that God has my back.

It might seem contradictory. Why make plans at all if half the time they are not going to work out? We make plans the same way we use some of the tools in this book: to manifest and influence our reality. They provide us with direction and purpose. They can guide our next steps. They help us feel less lost. Plans focus us. They give us feedback when they work out or when they don't. If we use them in a measurable way (which I will describe), we can keep taking stock to see if we are getting where we want to go – achieving our goals – or if we need to make tweaks in the plan. Just like your vision board and collage of yourself, your Life Plan will be something you review and keep present in your daily life. It is a living and breathing document that will change and morph as you add and subtract to it.

Making a plan is also a practice. It is not a static form that you fill out and forget about. We will start building it here. Your ongoing task is to review, revise, and update it as often as needed or wanted. It is a mirror for you of your progress. Let's see what we have learned so far that can be incorporated into your plan.

Elements of Your Life Plan

I hope that you created a vision board to get visuals on what you want to manifest. If you haven't done this exercise, it may actually be the first element of your Plan. We will get to how to structure it.

I have given you advice and suggestions for practices that will promote your healing and recovery. I bet some of them resonated with you and some did not at all. That is okay. You want to start with those that resonated. You can also start with ones you are curious about or that seem like a worthwhile experiment. Don't waste time with the ones that left you cold, for now. They are there if you get curious in the future.

The practices I've encouraged you to begin and integrate in your life are: Mindfulness and Meditation, Gratitude and Forgiveness, Prayer, Grounding, Prioritizing and Managing your Time, Self-Care, Asking for Help, and Manifesting. If you were already practicing some of these before you even picked up this book, you can put them in your Life Plan if you want to increase how much or how often you are doing them. Otherwise, keep on, keeping on with them.

You do not need to create a Life Plan that uses every single practice. This book is designed to help you decrease your overwhelm, not increase it. I would never advise you to suddenly start up seven new things. Instead choose two – or at most three – that you are ready to do. Remember to do, not try. Or to quote Yoda, "Do. Or do not. There is no try." What are you willing to do starting today? These are the actions we are going to use to create your Life Plan.

First, I will show you what we are going to do with each practice to make it into a plan of action for you.

How to Build Your Life Plan

If your reason for buying this book was to stop feeling so overwhelmed by your life after divorce, know that this is a great overall goal. There isn't exactly a short and sweet remedy for that. In order to help to decrease your feelings of overwhelm, we have to break it down into simple activities that you can do which can be measured. The reason we want to be able to measure them is to see if they are working. If you do them, you want to see if they produce the results you wanted. We call these specific activities the Objectives. This means they are the steps you are going to take to reach your goal.

When I decided to run a marathon, I didn't find a race, sign up for it, show up the day of the race, and run 26.2 miles. I created a very specific Marathon Running Plan, with the help of my coach. In my Running Plan, I broke down what I needed to do into bite-size bits so that by the time I got to race day, I knew I was going to be able to finish it. For instance, I started with one mile runs, moved up to three mile runs, eventually did weekly ten mile runs, then longer and longer training runs as race day approached. I trained myself into being a marathon runner. We want to train you into being a single-and-loving-it person by taking step-by-step measures to get there. Here is how we do this.

First, we figure out the overall goal that you'd like to achieve. In this case, we will use the goal: to decrease feelings of overwhelm. Next, we choose from the list of practices which ones to start with. Let's say we start with Prioritizing. Our measurable Objectives might read like this:

✓ I will make a list of ten things I need to do once a week.

✓ I will use the Time Management grid with my list once a week.

✓ I will accomplish all ten things by the end of the day Saturday.

In this example, we have one goal and three measurable Objectives. At the end of the day on Saturday, it is easy to look at your goal and answer the questions, "Did this work?" "Did I do this?" "If I didn't do this, what were the barriers?" Suppose you discover that making a list of ten To Dos and attempting to do them actually increases the feelings of overwhelm. That is feedback. That tells you it is too much. Maybe you should start with two things. Or you could give yourself a daily list with two things. The feedback allows you to adjust the objectives to make them workable. We want to build a plan that guides you to the successful achievement of your goals.

When you have a specific Objective, it gives you a clear direction to go. That, in and of itself, can be helpful in managing overwhelm. Instead of having a mind full of all the millions of things that need addressing, focus on a limited number with a defined plan. This can provide relief.

Here are more examples, since this may feel unnatural or weird at first. Therapists and coaches both do this with their clients but may use different words.

If we stick with the same goal to decrease feelings of overwhelm, we might use other practices and have Objectives that look like this:

✓ I will meditate for ten minutes every morning.

✓ I will say a prayer first thing in the morning, once during the day, and before I go to bed at night.

✓ I will take a hot bath after work on Wednesday night.

✓ I will use the grounding techniques every time I feel anxiety that is higher than a 5 on a 1 – 10 scale.

If you haven't done any of the practices in this book yet, your objective might simply be, "I will choose one practice from this book and begin to do it by next Monday."

You want to write these objectives down in a list – as I have shown in the example – to remember what they are and to check on them in whatever interval you determine.

Review Your Results and Change Your Objectives

If you review your results, it will help you track your progress and will inform you on what is and isn't working. To do this, you will review your Life Plan regularly. How often depends on what targets you have set for yourself. If your Objectives have weekly time frames, you would review it weekly. If they are daily, you would do it daily. It is okay to have daily, weekly, monthly, or even yearly targets. Keep in mind that this is not about giving yourself another reason to be overwhelmed. This is a guide for you to structure your healing activities and not another To Do.

When you review your progress, you want to notice if the Objective worked. If it did and you have accomplished it, do you want to change, increase, or decrease it? If you took a hot bath on Wednesday night and noticed that you felt great on Thursday but by Monday you were already stressed out again, you might want to increase that Objective and say that you will take a hot bath on Wednesday night after work and on Sunday afternoon. Play with what works. Experiment. Use your results to inform what you do next. Always remember that the key to practices working is to keep practicing them.

Some practices need to be mastered more fully before they will begin to produce results that you can see or like. If you do not feel calmer and have been meditating for ten minutes a day for a week, this is to be expected. Meditation usually takes a much longer time to master. In fact, many times it can increase feelings of discomfort at first as we become more aware of what we are feeling and thinking during our sitting time. Set your expectations gently, and know that we always want changes, particularly in our emotional states, to happen on a much faster time frame than they do. Some of the internal and external changes you want in your life right now may take six months to a year to manifest. This is not about magically making it all turn out right. This is about what we do during the process. How we manage ourselves and our lives while we heal. I like to describe our emotional states as being similar to weather systems. Sometimes it's raining and lightning is striking all around us. Other times, it's so windy it feels like we will be blown over. We have no control over the weather. We do have control over what we do during the storm. Knowing that storms pass – that emotions change rapidly – can help you hold on during the worst of it. Your objectives will give you something to do while it thunders and lightnings inside you.

Do not be tempted to change objectives if you don't get immediate results for these reasons. You want to check in on them at regular intervals but at the same time, give yourself a longer time to determine whether they need to be totally abandoned or replaced.

 ## FINAL EXERCISE

Your final exercise is to create your own Life Plan. I hope you have some new awareness about yourself and some goals and objectives you want to achieve with practices that help.

In your journal or on your computer, create a Life Plan. You can use the below format or make one up that you like.

My Life Plan

My Goal is: [Fill in the blank]. Make your goal big and general, like decreasing overwhelm or increasing peacefulness.

My Objectives are: I will [fill in what practice you will do] every [fill in week, day, month] for [add amount of time.] Do not create more than three Objectives. That's enough for now.

Post your Life Plan where you can see it regularly. Review it based on the time frames you have set for yourself. Update as needed. Celebrate your successes. Give yourself a reward each time you review an Objective and see that you have accomplished it. If you meditated every morning for a week, buy yourself a bouquet of flowers to celebrate. You could even meditate on them for the next week.

In Closing

I am rooting for you. I made it through this horrible, dark patch of my life. I know you can. I know that you can come out with renewed enthusiasm and a robustly healed heart. I would love to hear about your successes or any feedback you have for me on my book. This is the end of the book but does not have to be the end of our work together. Go to my Thank You page for information on how.

If you found value in this book and have learned new things about yourself, you can practice gratitude by writing a review of it on Amazon. I am deeply grateful for the opportunity to share my words with you.

Remember to continue to practice imperfectly! Don't Try! Do!!

THANK YOU

Congratulations! You are amazing! The fact that you've gotten to this point in my book tells me you are committed to pulling yourself up and flying forward! You can find a free self-assessment checklist on my website at www. marshavaughn.com, which you can use to evaluate where you are emotionally this week and to track your progress going forward.

CONTACT ME: I'd love to hear about your progress and how you are doing on your goals for your future. Please reach me at marsha@marshavaughn.com or on my Facebook page.

LET'S TALK: In real life: If you are interested in setting up a one-on-one call with me, please shoot me an email. Put "Flying" in the subject line. I will get you on my calendar for a call as soon as possible.

Until then, please accept a virtual hug!!

Marsha

ACKNOWLEDGMENTS

This book has been a long time in the making. There were lots of lessons and practices I needed to learn before I could step into the identity of the author of a book about recovering from divorce. Many people helped along the way.

I would never have started – let alone written it – without the unwavering support and brilliance of Angela E. Lauria. I want to thank the entire Author Incubator team. Thanks to Rae Guyn for keeping me on track with my deadlines. Maggie McReynolds was awesome as my editor and helped me see that I could do this. All of the other authors incubating alongside me were sources of inspiration, wisdom, and courage. Special thanks to Heather Russell for bringing me onto the team and for her deep listening. This network of brilliant and generous people pushed me through and supported me as I stepped into my new identity of author.

To the Morgan James Publishing team: Special thanks to David Hancock, CEO & Founder for believing in me and my message. To my Author Relations Manager, Bonnie Rauch, thanks for making the process seamless and easy. Many more thanks to everyone else, but especially Jim Howard, Bethany Marshall, and Nickcole Watkins.

For unwavering support and trust in me as her coach in so many situations, I am grateful to Tish Leona Silva. We went through many hard passes together. As I was teaching her, I was learning just as much.

My sisters and brothers, Claudia Terry, Sarah Lowther, Eldred Mowery, Jr., and Evan Mowery are in my heart every day. They were all along for the ride during my marriage and divorce with unfaltering support, even when they could see me going off the deep end. They have all also shown me how love-filled marriages can be.

The person who coached me through my fears of home-lessness and provided an example of how I could be a home-owner on my own was my dear friend and neighbor, Margo Dean. She taught me how to live with dogs, which has filled my life with love ever since. She also inspired me to become a marathon runner, which probably saved my husband's life.

To my friends Valerie Bluemel, Lucy Ames, and Lisa Mitchell, I say thanks for teaching me to be enthusiastic and to have fun. All of my fellow dancers and musicians in the zydeco dance community gave me a vehicle in which to express my joy. You also gave me a new practice, partner dancing, that I will never be able to perfect!

Without my therapist, Sandy Dibbell-Hope, I would likely still be watching re-runs of Law & Order. She stuck with me even when I yelled at her that there was no way I was going to take anti-depressants. She recommended many of the practices that I later incorporated into my life.

My friends in Twelve Step programs, both the Al-Anon Family Groups and Alcoholics Anonymous, taught me so much and were there with me through it all. I learned to Keep It Simple, to take life One Day at a Time and to Let Go and Let God among a multitude of other lessons. I hear their words of wisdom come out of my mouth daily. In the spirit of anonymity, I do not share their names but they know who they are.

To Thich Nhat Hahn, Pema Chodron, and Reverend Eloise Oliver – my spiritual teachers – I am deeply indebted for showing me the light. With each of them I have had lasting and inspiring in-person moments that convinced me that inner peace is not only possible but transmittable to others.

Finally, to you, my dear reader, I bow. I am grateful for your trust and interest. Without you, my service would be meaningless. All blessings to you!

ABOUT THE AUTHOR

Marsha Vaughn is a Licensed Clinical Social Worker in California. She is an author, life coach, clinical supervisor, professional trainer, and public speaker. She specializes in helping people who are dealing with overwhelm and loss. In her professional practice, she has helped people feel more empowered, focused, and competent. She has spent the past 15 years serving some of the hardest clients to serve. She supported youth in the foster care system to emancipate and reunite with family members or to launch lives of their own without family support; she facilitated teams who provided mental health services to families and youth in extreme mental health crises; and she assisted people with severe and persistent mental illness who were homeless to become welcome members of the community. Whether working with a professional as a clinical supervisor or providing direct services, Marsha works to help people in crisis recover, rebuild, and create the sustainable lives that they envision for themselves.

Marsha is trained in Motivational Interviewing, Trauma-Informed Care, Dialectical Behavioral Therapy, and Collaborative Problem Solving. She uses these and other therapeutic skills to provide motivational coaching focused on producing the results her clients want, both quickly and effectively. She has used these skills in the non-profit arena and is excited to take them into the larger community to support newly divorced people transition back to a life of peace and pleasure with her individualized coaching program.

Marsha lives with her two small dogs, Henry and Ellie, in Richmond, California. She enjoys the natural beauty and cultural diversity of the San Francisco Bay area and can often be found hiking with her dogs, gardening, attending music festivals, or zydeco dancing.

Website: marshavaughn.com

Email: marsha@marshavaughn.com

FB: Marsha-Vaughn-LCSW-Life-Coach-1639244979515788

SOURCES AND PERMISSIONS

I offer my grateful appreciation and acknowledgment of the following for their inspiring materials, which helped me on my journey.

Name It & Frame It: An Overview of Transitions, by Donna L. Mills, MA & Andrus Family Fund

7 Habits of Highly Effective People, by Steven R. Covey

There's A Hole in My Sidewalk: The Romance of Self Discovery, by Portia Nelson

Morgan James
Speakers Group

We connect Morgan James published
authors with live and online events
and audiences who will benefit
from their expertise.

CPSIA information can be obtained
at www.ICGtesting.com
Printed in the USA
LVHW032012111218
600083LV00005B/340